HISTORIC SHIPWRECKS
OF WALES

HISTORIC SHIPWRECKS OF WALES

Dilys Gater

Gwasg Carreg Gwalch

First edition: 1992
New edition: 2008
© Text: Dilys Gater

ISBN: 978-1-84524-086-8

Cover design: Sian Parri

First published in 1992 by Gwasg Carreg Gwalch
12 Iard yr Orsaf, Llanrwst, Wales LL26 0EH
☏ 01492 642031   ▤ 01492 641502

New edition published in 2008 by Llygad Gwalch,
Ysgubor Plas, Llwyndyrys, Pwllheli, Gwynedd LL53 6NG
☏ 01758 750432   ▤ 01758 750438
✆ books@carreg-gwalch.com   Website: www.carreg-gwalch.com

With love to Wendy, a gallant survivor,
and to all the other people who were there
when I needed them.

Author's Note

I am greatly indebted to the writers and historians who have covered all the ground dealt with in this book so thoroughly and in such detail. Without their expertise and years of personal research and enthusiasm, it would not be possible even to attempt to try and write a book of this nature.

Once again I would also like to acknowledge my gratitude to Wendy Lynne Hughes, who as usual provided a mine of information; and to my publisher, Myrddin ap Dafydd who provided whatever I asked for, as well as much appreciated encouragement.

Contents

Introduction

Shipwreck! Howling wind in the broken spars, while the waves thunder in clouds of spray across the half-submerged deck; screams of the victims as they are sucked into the vortex of dark water; looming rocks waiting like fangs to sink themselves into the helpless vessel. These are the ingredients of countless tales of the sea, from the story of Alexander Selkirk's *Robinson Crusoe* existence as a castaway on a desert island to the dark moment when the *Titanic* struck an iceberg in the freezing waters of the Atlantic.

There is something particularly significant about shipwrecks. They seem to be fateful happenings, acts of providence which reveal just how puny man is, and how futile are his efforts to pit himself against the elements. But paradoxically, the deeds which are done on such occasions of desperation and disaster can be those of heroic dimensions.

Wales is not often thought of as a maritime nation, far less as the scene of thrilling and dramatic shipwrecks. But one look at a map marking wrecks which have occurred in just the area round the Great Orme, for instance, can be very revealing.

Close round the coast, the *Jane Tudor*, the *Phoenix*, the *Britannia* and the *Morning Star* were only a few of the vessels which came to grief. And they were not just pleasure boats which floundered on a Saturday afternoon's sailing in the bay. The *Jane Tudor* for instance was an American barque of 345 tons, which came to grief on her maiden

8

voyage from Baltimore to Liverpool in 1847, carrying a cargo of corn and flour. She was wrecked, it was recorded at the time, 'in Hell's Mouth on the west side of Greatormeshead'. But there is no mention of the crew having perished, and the vessel herself was to survive the disaster. Wreck and contents were auctioned at Conwy, and were sold by the purchaser to two Conwy businessmen, who repaired her and returned her to the sea, this time under a Beaumaris registration.

The *Jane Tudor* became a part of Welsh maritime history. She sailed between Conwy and Montreal, and the historian Ivor Wynne Jones records: 'it was claimed that no vessel carried as much timber . . . for the constructing of modern Llandudno during the boom years 1850-70.'

The history of Wales is just as thrilling, just as dramatic, just as filled with tragedy, heroism and romance if we confine it only to the coasts, to the great cliffs, the hidden caves, the bays where the surf laps on fine sand, or thunders on dark nights. Wales has been on familiar terms with many larger-than-life figures of the sea: like wreckers and smugglers, many ghosts of whom still haunt the paths down to the sea when the moon is obscured.

According to legend, King Arthur's ship, *Caswennan*, was wrecked in Swnt Enlli, the narrow, turbulent stretch of water between Enlli (*Bardsey*) and the mainland, and this romantic episode is still remembered in the names of Ffrydiau Caswennan and Creigiau Caswennan (*Caswennan Strait and Caswennan Rocks*). Another legendary hazard lurking beneath the waves to bring death and destruction to ships is the rock known as Maen Mellt (*the Stone of Lightning*), which lies out at sea just under the level of the water near Bodferin, Llŷn.

Apart from being a hazard in the way of ordinary rocks which are submerged and can catch the unwary vessel that might run aground on them, this one, according to local tradition, is much more sinister. It has been claimed that the geological structure of the rock causes it to attract lightning — and also to play havoc with ships' compasses. Evidence of its deadly nature, whether because of the lightning, or interfering with compasses magnetically or simply being there, lie in its record of wrecks. In 1802, the *Lovely* met her fate here; the *Luther* sank on it in 1884 en route to Newfoundland, while the *Casgin* went down in 1814.

While there are no records of Spanish galleons from the scattered

Armada fleet being spectacularly wrecked off the coasts of Wales, legend fills in the details for us. Local tradition has it that two of these vessels did in fact come aground on the Llŷn Peninsula, and that, far from treating the sailors as enemies, the people welcomed them and made haste to provide them with all the comforts of home. The results of this unlimited hospitality, it is claimed, account for the fact that many of the poeple still living in the area, are dark-haired, dark-skinned and bear a great resemblance to the natives of Spain!

The wrecks of Wales must surely include some of the most bizarre stories ever to be told about such disasters, and we will be hearing of many of them within these pages. That of the *Villa* is a good example: a Spanish ship carrying coal from Liverpool to Le Havre, she ran aground at Porth Colman on the same night the *Royal Charter* met her terrible end in the great hurricane of 1859. (See Chapter 18). One of the crew was drowned, but the remainder struck fear into the hearts of the local people, who ventured to the wreck the following morning to see whether they could be of any assistance — or possibly, to see what they could make off with. The locals were met with the sight of a terrifying crowd of rough foreigners, swords buckled to their belts, who looked as though they might cut a few throats at the slightest provocation.

Some sort of understanding must have been reached, however, between these swarthy foreigners and the locals. The dead seaman was buried at Llangwnnad Church, and we can imagine the fearsome crew his former comrades made as they clustered at the graveside. Unfortunately, the grave had been dug far too short, so one of the Spaniards jumped onto the top of the body, to ensure that it went all the way down. The problem of how to lift him out afterwards was solved by the Vicar, who, being a strong man, was able to obligingly pull him back up from the grave.

Further confusion between survivors and those who helped them to survive, took place when the *Sorrento*, en route from Liverpool to New Orleans in October, 1870, ran onto the rocks at Porth Tŷ Mawr, Llŷn. One unfortunate sailor who tried to get a line to the shore, was drowned, and the rest of the crew waited for the tide to ebb, and then were able to reach the shore with no trouble. But when they staggered to the nearest farm — Tŷ Mawr — they were met by the son of the house holding a gun in a business-like manner. The family were convinced these men were the forerunners of an Irish invasion, and since they could not speak a word of English, the Captain, a very wet and weary man, was forced to demonstrate by means of three matches stuck into a matchbox to resemble a three-masted ship, that they were survivors who had been wrecked!

One of the most spine-chilling disasters ever to happen off the coast of Wales took place near the great stretch of sand at Porth Neigwl, which is known as 'Hell's Mouth' because it has been the downfall of so many ships. This wide curve faces south-west, and in bad weather, the Atlantic waves run in right to the shore. It appears a good place for captains to shelter, but many who tried to do so were driven, unsuspecting, onto the sandbanks, or else were caught between the two headlands with the land in front and the wind at the ship's back, and no chance of escape.

It was in 1629 when a French ship, lured by the false lights of wreckers who had lit bonfires on Mynydd Rhiw, came to grief on the rocks here. The vessel was carrying many of the French nobility, who were wearing rich clothing and many jewels. It is difficult to believe the stories that the wreckers swarmed aboard as the vessel ran aground and attacked the survivors, killing men and women indiscriminately, and not only slaughtering them but cutting off their fingers and ears to seize their jewels. Two of the wreckers paid for their crimes at the rope's end and we turn from these black pages of Wales' maritime history to the more inspiring tales of Welsh shipwreck.

There have been great rescues and escapes, so miraculous that we would never believe the stories except that we know they really happened. In the early nineteenth century, for instance, two ferry-boats, the Tal-y-foel and the Abermenai ferries, sank in the same year off Anglesey. Only one man survived each disaster — and he was the same man, Hugh Williams of Bodowyr! Not a passenger ships' captains would have been too enthusiastic about taking on board afterwards, we can imagine.

Captains, ship-owning families, pioneers of maritime reform, modest heroes like Richard Evans, former coxwain of the Moelfre lifeboat who achieved the remarkable distinction of being awarded the Gold Medal of the R.N.L.I. not once, but twice for gallantry at sea — Wales has seen them all. She can even boast her own sons in the world of piracy. Not only the great Henry Morgan came from Wales — so too did Captain Bartholomew Roberts, whose spectacular career on the high seas was equalled only by his personal idiosyncracies like drinking only tea, insisting on 'lights out' on his ships at eight p.m. and allowing no females on board ship on pain of death.

These were the great names which have passed into history but the heroes and heroines of these tales of drama at sea were often simple people who lived humbly, who were willing to risk their own lives when a stricken ship was on the rocks, in an effort to pluck sodden and scarcely-still-human bodies from the fangs of the deep. There are even small heroes of the animal kingdom who have played their part, as we shall see, in courageous rescue attempts which deserve to be remembered.

A dark night when the wind is howling and the elements are thundering outside, shaking the window-glass, while the light flickers ominously and there is creaking in the timbers of the room where you are sitting — this is the best setting for these stories of the drama, terror, romance and tragedy of Welsh shipwrecks.

Chapter One
Early Wrecks

There have been wrecks off the coasts of Wales since the beginning of history. Many traders who sailed in Roman times to this far-off corner of the known world, driven by their greed for the precious ore from Wales' mines, probably met their end beneath these remote cliffs in the same way that Viking raiders might well have done in later centuries. So long as there were ships, of whatever sort, passing the Welsh coast or trying to land, then sooner or later, by accident or because the custom of wrecking — luring ships to their doom and plundering the spoils — dates back to the dawn of time, there would have been wrecks.

But the very early wrecks off the coasts of Wales cannot be established as proven fact, and have passed into the realms of legend, tradition and folk-lore. One story is told, for instance, of a terrible storm which drove a vessel onto the rocks in the Cardiganshire parish of Llanina near Newquay in western Dyfed, some time during the early eighth century. A local fisherman, his wife and his daughter, were among those who rowed out not once, but several times to rescue those aboard the doomed ship.

Nobody knew who the survivors were since they spoke in a foreign language, but when a monk arrived to see what assistance he could render, he was able to tell the good fisherfolk that the men they had saved from the sea were no less than a royal personage — King Ina of

England — and, we can only suppose, his attendants and retinue.

In his gratitude to the people, the rescued monarch is said to have built a church which was called Llan Ina, or Ina's Church. The parish still bears the name Llanina, though the original church apparently stood some way off-shore where a landmark called Cerrig Ina (*Ina's stones*) commemorates the event.

It is not surprising that the stories of the early wrecks only exist now as hearsay and folk-tales. The modern scientific methods of keeping in touch with ships at sea, of being able to contact the owners if disaster should occur, of recording and identifying a wreck, did not exist. Logs of stricken vessels were often lost with the ship, and it was quite possible that a ship would come to be wrecked purely because its officers had no idea of where they were. Often, too, a vessel that was wrecked might have broken up in a heavy sea so that there was very little left as evidence of what had happened by the time the inhabitants of these remote areas of coastline were aware that the wreck had occurred.

Communications were primitive, to say the least, and there were very few newspapers or methods of circulating information between different parts of the country until developments began to be made in these directions during the seventeenth and eighteenth centuries. In addition, so far as many parts of sea-faring Wales were concerned, there was a long and well-established tradition that if they should occur, wrecks of whatever sort were nothing less than welcome gifts from the sea.

In Pembrokeshire, for instance, it was not only the local people who indulged in 'hanging out false lights to decoy the wandering mariner in order to benefit from his misfortunes', as the historian Richard Fenton noted in 1811. Local wreckers were enthusiastically aided and abetted by the local customs officers! And even those in high office who might have frowned on such practices as criminal and immoral did not always set an example. There is one tale of a clergyman who was conducting a church service in Marloes when news arrived that a ship had just been wrecked under the cliffs nearby. As the congregation got to its feet in a body to head for the wreck and help itself to whatever plunder might be waiting, the clergyman pleaded with them for 'moderation in all things', but added that he felt they ought to give him a head start since he was no longer so sprightly as he used to be.

This tradition that wrecks — or even vessels which might be

persuaded to be wrecked — were there purely to provide a lucrative source of income and profit for the Welsh peasantry, goes back many centuries. In their own way, the Welsh coasts were just as notorious as the coasts of Cornwall, as the haunt of wreckers and smugglers. Amazingly enough, the coasts of Wales have also been dangerously populated with pirates — particularly during the seventeenth century — and slavers too were not unknown here.

It was an ironic twist of fortune that ships which were to sail to and from Liverpool on the much-reviled 'triangular run' during the 1700s, making immense fortunes for those concerned in the slave trade — cramming their holds with black slaves on the West Coast of Africa and selling them at fantastic profit in the Americas — often assisted the Welsh peasants to a more luxurious lifestyle when they were wrecked, either by accident or because the wreckers had been abroad with their false lights, on the Welsh coast. Possibly fate was compensating the coastal dwellers for what had gone on during the perilous days of the Stuarts, when Arab slave traders stood off the Welsh coast and made daring attacks even on relatively large towns like Holyhead.

In 1631, for instance, the zealous gentleman who bore the impressive title of admiral of the king's ships in the Irish Sea, was apparently making a report as to the actions he had been taking to hunt down the pirates who were terrorising the coast. But even as he sat writing in Holyhead, 150 people were captured almost under his nose, destined for the white slave markets of North Africa.

It is not surprising, then, that these coasts can boast few, if any wrecks which can be conclusively dated before about the seventeenth century, even though large numbers of ships were almost certainly lost before this time. But however many wrecks occurred, each one would have been the scene of incidents of great drama to those who were present. Tales, eye-witness accounts of what had really happened, often passed into local folk-lore as we have seen, and sometimes the story is all that is left for the interested enquirer to uncover. Sometimes though, the stories are reinforced by evidence — the sight of skeletal spars revealed by a low tide, or the now yellowing accounts in the newspapers of that time, as the disaster was recorded while events were happening. Sometimes the wreck holds more thrilling secrets — like the one described in this next chapter.

Chapter Two
"The Dollar Ship"

In the best romantic tradition, the coast of Wales is the setting for one of the world's most tantalizing mysteries involving hidden treasure. Somewhere along the wild stretch of sand at Rhosili Bay, on the tip of the Gower Peninsula, lies — if we can believe the evidence — a fortune in seventeenth century silver dollars, made by the Spaniards from the silver of Peru, lost here when the "Dollar Ship" carrying them was sunk in the late 1600s, and largely still undiscovered and unclaimed.

The name of the vessel which sank does not appear to have been recorded, and the date of the wreck is also uncertain. No-one can say what happened to the ship, and no official record of the wreck exists, but it is generally believed to have taken place between 1640 and the end of the century. According to local tradition, the ship was a Spanish galleon which had been entrusted to carry the dowry of Catherine of Braganza, the Portuguese princess who married Charles II, to her husband.

History — as opposed to tradition — make no mention of Catherine's dowry being so spectacularly lost off the Welsh coast, but the one thing which is certain is that wherever it was destined for, an immense fortune in silver Spanish coins was scattered as some doomed ship broke up, and the bulk of it still lies hidden on or around Rhosili Bay, buried deep in the clutches of the sands and the surf, along with the remains of the wrecked hulk.

It is possible that there were up to 400,000 coins and almost as soon as the wreck had settled, there were attempts to try and seize the treasure. The sands on this part of the coast can shift dramatically with the action of the tides, which can be treacherous — nevertheless it is claimed locally that a smuggler called Mr Mansel of Henllys braved the dangers to break into the wreck and remove most of the coins before disappearing from the country.

This was in defiance of the ancient right of the Lord of the Manor to lay claim to the treasure, and the action aroused a great deal of bad feeling between the people of Rhosili and those of Mr Mansel's home parish of Llanddewi. Indeed, it is even claimed in other local tales that Mr Mansel did not get away with his daring crime but was murdered and robbed of the silver, after which his body was hidden somewhere in the bay.

It is said that he haunts Rhosili Bay and that his ghost drives a black coach — known as the Spectre Chariot of Rhosili Sands — along the beach at midnight, drawn by four grey horses.

Events in the early nineteenth century were to reveal, however, that even if Mr Mansel had managed to make off with part of the silver, he had not touched the bulk of the treasure. On two occasions, unusual activities of the tide shifted the sand briefly to reveal enormous deposits of silver coins and other relics — as well as what was left of the wreck itself — before covering them again.

The first of these incidents took place in 1807, when after a particularly low equinoxial tide, the decayed remains of the wreck could be seen out in the bay. Several local men scrambled to the spot to dig for the silver which popular conviction firmly believed was still there. They saw huge piles of coins revealed by the sand and the tide, and they tried to gather up as much of the treasure as they could before the returning tide drove them from the spot.

One man, William Bevan, was so anxious not to miss out on this golden (or rather, silver!) opportunity to join the moneyed classes, that he stripped off his trousers and tied the legs together in order to make a sort of bag into which the coins could be thrown for easy transportation. The sum total the men managed to collect between them before the tide drove them back and the wreck disappeared again, was about twelve pounds' worth of silver dollars and half dollars, as well as assorted pewter and a cask of iron wire.

The treasure was seen no more — until the year 1833, after a roaring gale along the coast threw back the sands to reveal the silver once again. Another group of local men happened to notice that there had been activity in the spot where the wreck was presumed to lie, and they hastened to start digging. Soon they were bringing up shovelfuls of dollars, but once again, the incoming tide prevented further exploration, the waves washing hundreds of silver coins from their shovels as they attempted to lift them from the water. Although they tried to mark the place with a buoy, it had disappeared by the next morning.

News of the discoveries quickly spread, however, and everyone in the vicinity rushed to Rhosili Bay to try and grab a share in the treasure, even going so far as to stake their claims on the sands in the best 'gold rush' tradition. Families set up camp on the beach and some even brought their own equipment — one Swansea group enterprisingly set up a makeshift coffer dam in which they could work. There was a good deal of quarrelling, and fights soon broke out, but in this atmosphere of frenzied excitement, the treasure-hunters did uncover further large numbers of dollars as well as other interesting relics, before the whole treasure site was once again entirely obscured by the sands and the sea.

Several cannon, cannon balls and pieces of old navigational instruments were saved from the wreck, and were afterwards prized as souvenirs by the local people, though most of the latter were, naturally enough, far more interested in the silver coins which were discovered. Those found on this second occasion when the wreck was visible were identified as dating between 1621 and 1665, from the reign of Philip IV of Spain. They were Spanish Pieces of Eight, minted at Potosi in Peru.

Apparently the "Dollar Ship" was not the only vessel carrying treasure to be wrecked in the bay. In view of the confusion over whether the "Dollar Ship" was actually transporting Catherine of Braganza's dowry to her husband, or whether the silver Spanish coins were on their way to a different destination, it has been suggested that the "Dollar Ship" might in fact have been another vessel entirely.

At Spaniard Rocks, near Burry Holmes Island to the north of Rhosili Sands, tradition has it that the survivors from the "Dollar Ship" scrambled ashore. A few coins have been found here over the years, but the evidence suggests that they were from another vessel, and it seems likely that there were at least two other galleons which ran into difficulties in the bay.

At Bluepool Corner, further up the coast, treasure discovered in the form of gold moidors and doubloons would appear to indicate that another ship carrying gold was wrecked near the spot, and it is known that a vessel carrying gold bullion probably met its end somewhere on the Burry Estuary. Most of the gold was apparently recovered, but this wreck of a galleon carrying bullion would help to explain away the various findings of gold coins in the vicinity.

It is not likely that the "Dollar Ship" was one and the same as this golden galleon, but one theory which has been put forward — notably by the writer George Edmunds, who has probably collected together more detailed information on the subject of the "Dollar Ship" than any other authority — is that the identity of the "Dollar Ship" might have been that of the one Spanish galleon known to have been wrecked in this area. The vessel was the *El Dorado*, which was apparently carrying £80,000 in gold and silver when she was reported sunk off Worms Head, to the south of Rhosili Bay, on 3rd October, 1691.

Could the "Dollar Ship" and the *El Dorado* have been the same vessel, and this simple fact have been distorted by tradition and local legend over the centuries? Perhaps the silver coins discovered in 1807 and 1833 were only a portion of the £80,000's worth of gold and silver that the vessel was carrying, and the rest still lies, as we have already mentioned, waiting to be discovered beneath the sands of Rhosili Bay.

Chapter Three
Tyger — Four-footed Hero

The bravery of animals during times of crisis, and their loyalty and devotion to their masters has been documented over and over. A goose called Jacob was awarded a golden collar in 1837, for instance, when he saved the Coldstream Guards from being attacked by cackling out a warning when the regiment was stationed in Canada. Many other birds too performed heroic feats, particularly when carrier pigeons were used to pass messages between ships at sea before the invention of radio. During World War I, many sailors who were wrecked owed their lives to these small birds, and it was not unusual for the pigeons to receive medals for their gallantry. The RSPCA version of the VC, a special one for animals, is known as the Dickin Medal.

But often, a small creature performing a loving service of devotion is not awarded any medal save the fond thoughts and remembrance of his master. Such a hero was Tyger, who willingly gave his life in a shipwreck off the Welsh coast in order to save the crew of his master's vessel.

The night of 17th September, 1819, was black with heavy fog. A ketch bound for Liverpool, feeling its way through the murk off the Anglesey coast, struck the dangerous Maen Piscar rock and almost immediately began to sink.

Since the fog was so thick, it was impossible for the crew of four to see the coastline, and they did not know which way to try to swim to save themselves. But the Captain's retriever, Tyger, barked eagerly, and appeared to be quite confident as to the direction in which they should swim. With the ship's boy clinging to his collar, the gallant animal struggled a quarter of a mile through the surf to reach safety.

But tired though the faithful dog was, he swam back to his master and the other survivors who were still clinging grimly to what wreckage there was, and trying to keep afloat. One of the men was in difficulties, and with the other two somehow managing to keep together and follow his lead, Tyger tugged the stricken seaman ashore by the collar of his jacket.

All four of the crew managed to escape drowning, thanks to the gallantry and faithfulness of one small dog. But the effort had been too much for Tyger, and he died exhausted in his master's arms there on the very shores of safety that they had struggled so hard to reach.

Other animals, dogs, cats, ships' pets of whatever kind, almost certainly performed similar deeds of heroism in the course of the long history of Welsh shipwrecks. But because few of such deeds were recorded — possibly no-one ever heard about the faithful animal's attempt to give assistance in the only way it felt it could — we do not know their stories.

As for Tyger, he was buried in the south-eastern corner of Penrhos Bay, on the cliff-top overlooking the sea which had been the scene of his heroic rescue. A stone to mark his grave was erected with the simple inscription:

'Tyger, September 17th, 1819.'

And there he rests.

Chapter Four

The Women of Mumbles Head

January 27, 1883, was one of the most tragic days in the whole history of the South Glamorgan coast. Losses of life from shipwrecks on that day reached a terrible total of 48 men, these being from several wrecks and not just from one vessel.

The portents of doom began when the SS *Agnes Jack* of Liverpool, on route to Llanelli with a cargo of silver bearing copper ore from Sardinia, went aground off the shore at Skysea early in the morning of 27 January, 1883.

One of the most fearful gales ever to occur along the Gower was in the process of blowing up, and hampered all rescue operations and efforts made by the local people to help the stricken ship. The eventual breaking of dawn light revealed that the crew were, in their desperation, trying to save themselves from the hungry sea by clinging to the rigging and the yardarm of the foremast. Five of the crew members had tried to escape in the ship's boat during the hours of darkness, but were later found beaten to death on the rocks of the foreshore.

The gale was by now so fierce that any attempt to get a line to the ship was doomed to failure, and as the tide came in, the spectators could only watch with horror while enormous waves, driven by the gale force winds, crashed over the ship. In full view of the spectators on the shore, the sailors were washed, one by one, from their frail perches of safety in the rigging, and disappeared into the angry seas.

Some men were still clinging to the yardarm, and further attempts were made to get a line to them, but at about midday, the mainmast itself crashed down and the sailors who were still alive were swallowed up in the turbulent sea, dying within minutes before the horrified gaze of those who were trying to help them.

Eighteen bodies were recovered over a period of time, mostly badly injured and mutilated by the rocks. The whole crew of the SS *Agnes Jack* perished in those few hours.

Partly as a result of this tragedy and the further tragedies which followed on the heels of the loss of the SS *Agnes Jack*, a new lifeboat station was established at Port Einon. On the first anniversary of the disaster, the secretary of the lifeboat station, Charles Bevan, composed a poem which was afterwards read out every year in commemoration of the event. Here, in the language of one of the men who experienced the drama and the tragedy himself, is what really took place:

In Memoriam
The Loss of the SS *Agnes Jack* January 27th 1883

It was a dark and stormy morn
Long ere the break of day
When cries of deep distress were heard
Across Port Einon Bay.

The Vill'gers quickly rose from bed
And hurried to the strand;
There shattered spars and broken boats
Were washed up on the sand.

And woeful cries borne by the wind
Distinctly they could hear;
Above the roaring of the sea,
Sad wails fell on the ear.

Yonder o'er Skysea rugged rocks
A mast-head light was seen,
And through the murky darkness there
That flickering light did gleam.

The wild waves seethed upon the shore,
And winds did howl and moan,
And from the mountain breakers rose
The angry spray and foam.

When dawned the day upon the scene
Out through the misty gloom,
The topmasts of a sunken ship
Above the waves did loom.

And in the rigging human forms
Were clinging for their lives,
We gazed with pity on them there,
For help we heard their cries.

Their ship had struck the fatal rocks
In the darkness of the night,
Upon a wild and dangerous coast,
For there's no beacon light.

Cast on an iron-bound lee-shore,
The rocks her sides did gore,
And eighteen men on board were doomed
To see their homes no more.

They sought for refuge in the mast,
And the shaking ropes they grip,
Whilst the raging billows swept the decks
Of that ill-fated ship.

In fragments high upon the beach,
Their every boat was cast,
And all the hope, poor souls, they had,
Was that frail breaking mast.

The coast-guards and the rocket crews,
Now did their duty brave,
But with their rockets and their lines,
Alas! they could not save.

A sorrowing crowd stood on the shore,
The tear filled many an eye,
Yet sympathy could not avail,
They all were doomed to die.

And good men offered prayers to God
For those in sore distress,
For all the powers of man were vain
To rescue them from death.

Small open boats upon the beach
There at Port Einon lay,
But these were useless in the waves
Of the foaming storm-lashed bay.

And men with hard and stony hearts
Were melted into tears,
While cries of those poor souls for help
Fell on their listening ears.

Five dreadful hours had passed away,
And still for help they cry,
No lifeboat to launch from the shore,
No arm to save was nigh.

Out in the surges clinging there
To that frail mast and rope,
They gazed upon the crowds on shore
Without a ray of hope.

Drenched and benumbed with wet and cold,
They saw each foaming wave,
That rolled in madness 'neath their feet,
And yawned their dreadful grave.

Some stripped the clothes from off their backs,
And shoes from off their feet,
While on the verge of death they stood,
Their certain doom to meet.

The shrouds are gone, the frail mast bends,
And it is breaking fast,
And now their prayers to God for help
Were heard above the blast.

A mountain wave broke on the mast,
Down in the surf it fell;
And oh! the sadness of that sight,
No human tongue can tell.

They battled with the raging waves,
In vain the shore to reach,
While scores of strong and willing men,
Stood helpless on the beach.

Huge waves o'er whelmed them and they sank,
So close, so near the shore;
Their languid cries were hushed in death —
Life's voyage now was o'er.

The gloom of death spread all around;
For them there tolled no bell;
The moaning of the wind and waves
Seemed like death's solemn knell.

Oh! had there been a lifeboat there
To breast the stormy main,
Those men might not have perished thus,
Imploring help in vain.

But thus they perished — thus they sank —
So very near the shore;
The *Agnes Jack* and her brave crew
'Shall plough the deep no more.'

In the teeth of this same furious gale, on 27th January 1883, another
vessel, the barque *Admiral Prinz Adalbert*, was driven towards
Mumbles Head, and in spite of being taken in tow by a Swansea tug in
two attempts to save her, she continued to drift nearer to the dangerous

rocks, as the storms snapped the 9-inch hawsers as though they were strands of cotton.

The Mumbles lifeboat was called out, but before help could arrive, the *Prinz Adalbert* had gone aground on the rocks below the lighthouse, her masts broken as though they were matchsticks. It seemed suicidal to launch the lifeboat in the face of such a gale, such mountainous seas and the storm more terrible than any in living memory, and some efforts were made to persuade the Coxwain not to try. He was told that conditions were 'hell, I tell you', to which he shouted above the blast: 'Well, hell it shall be.'

After three attempts, the lifeboat was launched on its brave and — some thought — foolhardy mission to the dying ship. It almost seemed as though the lifeboat would never make it to the side of the stranded vessel; the watchers on the shore must have feared with every gigantic wave and every new shriek of the gale that its gallant crew had gone down on their errand of mercy. But though it proved impossible to get close to the *Prinz Adalbert*, the lifeboat managed to anchor about 30 yards away and got a line across to the stricken ship.

Two men were taken off in a perilous rescue attempt, but even while a third was being transferred to the lifeboat, its anchor cable parted and the lifeboat was overturned in enormous waves. The crew were scattered into the water, and though the lifeboat remained afloat, so badly damaged that she was later taken away from the scene by a tug, it was impossible to try and get back on board as the seas were making her buck and drag against the rocks like a mad thing.

The only hope of the lifeboat crew was to try and make for the shore, and although miraculously, only four of them and one member of the crew of the *Prinz Adalbert* perished, the survivors were all grievously injured from their ordeal in the waves and many had broken limbs — one had suffered the crushing of both his legs.

But this was a day of heroism which was celebrated by several writers who felt the occasion called for the most appreciative wielding of their pens. In particular, the efforts of the two daughters of the lighthouse keeper, Abraham Ace, who risked their lives in a gallant attempt to save some of the survivors by going up to their armpit into the boiling sea themselves, received universal acclaim, and was the subject of a narrative poem written in 1883 by a gentleman called Clement Scott titled 'The Women of Mumbles Head'. This dramatic ballad became one of the standard pieces in the repertoires of 'elocutionists' who performed 'parlour poetry' in many Edwardian and later social gatherings.

But let us first hear the official report, in brisk journalistic prose, taken from the newspaper *The Cambrian* which recorded that:

> 'For some days previously the wind had been strong and gusty but about five o-clock it gathered up its strength and blew with great fury and accompanied ever and anon by showers of hail and rain. On the sea coast it expanded all its power and as a result we have to record an awful tale of loss of human life. The first intimation that reached the town was a telegram which was posted up both at the Harbour Office and the Cambrian Office soon after 12.20 p.m. to the effect that a Dantzic barque had gone ashore off the Mumbles Head, losing one of her crew and worse still that in the course of a gallant effort to save life, the Mumbles lifeboat had been stove in and six of her crew had perished. (In fact, four crew members died.)
>
> The lives of two of the lifeboat's crew were saved by Miss Ace, the daughter of the lighthouse keeper who went down to the rocks, up to her waist in water and threw her shawl to the sinking men and so drew them ashore.'

Filling in more melodramatic detail, let us now hear Mr Clement Scott's ballad:

The Women of Mumbles Head
Clement Scott

Bring novelists, your notebook! bring, dramatist, your pen!
And I'll tell you a simple story of what women do for men.
It's only a tale of a lifeboat, of the dying and the dead,
Of a terrible storm and shipwreck, that happened off Mumbles Head.
Maybe you have travelled in Wales, sir, and know it north and south;
Maybe you are friends with the natives that dwell at Oystermouth;
It happened, no doubt, that from Bristol you've crossed in a casual way
And have sailed your yacht in the summer, in the blue of Swansea Bay.

28

Well, it isn't like that in the winter, when the lighthouse stands alone,
In the teeth of Atlantic breakers, that foam on its face of stone,
It wasn't like that when the hurricane blew, and the storm bell tolled or when
There was news of a wreck, and the lifeboat, and a desperate cry for men.
When in the work did the coxwain shirk? a brave old salt was he!
Proud to the bone of as four strong lads as ever had tasted the sea,
Welshmen all to the lungs and loins, who, about that coast 'twas said,
Had saved some hundred lives a piece — at a shilling or so a head!

It didn't go well with the lifeboat! 'twas a terrible storm that blew,
And it snapped the rope in a second that was flung to the drowning crew;
And then the anchor parted — 'twas a tussle to keep afloat!
But the father stuck to the rudder, and the boys to the brave old boat.
Then at last on the poor doom'd lifeboat a wave broke mountains high!
'God help us now!' said the father, 'it's over my lads goodbye.'
Half of the crew swam shoreward! half to the sheltered caves,
But father and sons were fighting death in the foam of the angry waves.

Up at the lighthouse window two women beheld the storm,
And saw in the boiling breakers a figure — a fighting form,
It might be a grey haired father, then the women held their breath,
It might be a fair haired brother, who was having a round with death;
It might be a lover, a husband whose kisses were on the lips
Of the women whose love is the life of men, going down to the sea in ships:
They had seen the launch of the lifeboat, they had seen the worst and more;
Then kissing each other, these women went down from the lighthouse
straight to the shore.

There by the rocks on the breakers these sisters, hand in hand,
Beheld once more that desperate man who struggled to reach the land.
'Twas only aid he wanted to help him across the wave
But what are a couple of women with only a man to save?
What are a couple of women? well more than three craven men
Who stood by the shore with chattering teeth refusing to stir — and then
Off went the women's shawls, sir, in a second they're torn and rent,
Then knotting them into a rope of love, straight into the sea they went!

'Come back!' cried the lighthouse keeper, 'For God's sake girls, come back!'
As they caught the waves on their foreheads, resisting the fierce attack.
'Come back!' moaned the greyhaired mother, as she stood by the angry sea,
'If the waves take you, my darlings, there's nobody left to me.'
'Come back!' said the three strong soldiers, who still stood faint and pale,
'You'll drown in the face of the breakers! You will fall if you brave the gale!'
'Come back!' said the girls, 'we will not! go tell it to all the town
We'll lose our lives, God willing, before that man shall drown.'

'Give one more knot to the shawls, Bess! Give one strong clutch of your hand!
Just follow me, brave, to the shingle, and we'll bring him safe to land!
Wait for the next wave, darling, only a minute more,
And I'll have him safe in my arms, dear, and we'll drag him safe to the shore.'
Up to the arms in water, fighting it breast to breast,
They caught and saved a brother alive! God bless us we know the rest —
Well many a heart beat stronger, and many a tear was shed,
And many a glass was tossed right off to the Women of Mumbles Head.

Ironically, the *Prinz Adalbert* survived her pounding by the gales, and at low tide the fifteen crew members who survived were able to be assisted ashore safely, though the vessel did break up the following day. But there was no further loss of life from this wreck. In commemoration of that terrible day, however, when the Ace girls were not the only ones who displayed a true spirit of gallantry and heroism, the RNLI's Silver Medal was awarded to the Coxwain of the Mumbles lifeboat, Jenkin Jenkins — who had lost two of his four sons in the crew, and seen the others badly injured — while the 'Women of Mumbles Head' — the Ace sisters — were given awards in gratitude by the German government.

To add to the total of deaths from shipwreck on this fateful day, there was a further tragedy when the 1058 ton steamer *James Gray* — having made efforts to seek shelter from the storm, as did many other vessels caught up in it — was seen to be in trouble off Nash, and the Porthcawl lifeboat was launched. Even with the Porthcawl lifeboat's assistance, however, she was still in severe difficulties, and the coastguards telegraphed a summons for the Mumbles lifeboat — unaware that the Mumbles lifeboat had already perished in the aid of the *Prinz Adalbert*.

In a scene of drama, the *James Gray* drifted with dragging anchors towards the fearful Tusker Rock, and after one of her cables parted in the gale, she disappeared shorewards. Nothing more was seen of this ship in the turmoil of the storm, but the flares of distress rockets. It was afterwards known, however, that she had gone aground on the reef and all 25 of her crew were lost. Perhaps if the Mumbles lifeboat had been able to come to the assistance of her fellow from Porthcawl, this vessel, or at least, some of her crew, might have been saved. But it was not to be, and the evening of 27 January 1883 closed mercifully on a day of much grief, shock and tragedy, as well as heroism and the best in the human spirit. It was not a day to be soon forgotten by any who had lived through it on the Gower coast.

Chapter Five
Smugglers and Wreckers

The dangers to shipping in past centuries were very great. Even in 1642, when plans were afoot for King Charles I to sail to Ireland, the merchants in Chester pointed out that 'Winde and waters (make) no difference betwixt the greatest King and the meanest subject.'

Seafaring was a hazardous occupation and few sailors lived into middle years and old age safely. Ships sometimes collided with rocks without assistance from wreckers, or ran aground to break up in thunderous surf. They collided with each other, ran into hurricanes or bad weather, or broke down because they were not properly maintained, or simply because they were too old to be at sea.

The most feared of the elements — even more than wind and waves — was fire, particularly in the days when vessels were made of wood. The old sailing ships were extremely vulnerable to the dangers of fire on board, and often fire could occur as a result of carrying a combustible or highly inflammable cargo, such as oil, cotton or coal.

It was recorded that the charts of the Welsh coasts were particularly inaccurate, and pointed out in William Morris' revised edition of his 'Plans of Harbours', that for every one vessel lost on the coast of Ireland, ten came to grief on the opposite coast of Wales.

Danger to ships from such chancy occurrences as a collision or bad weather, was not enough, however, for the various gangs of wreckers who inhabited parts of the Welsh coast over the centuries, and who needed to be certain that the cargoes of stricken vessels would end up in their own hands, so that they could enrich themselves at the expense of the poor souls aboard.

Near Rhosneigr in Anglesey, home since the late 1770s of a thriving ship-building industry, gangs of wreckers called the Wreckers of Crigyll flourished at various periods, particularly during the Eighteenth Century. They became notorious for their activities at luring ships to their doom and then plundering them, so much so that long after the original 'gang' which gave these wreckers their name had met its fate, wrecks were still being attributed to its activities.

On 30 October 1867, *The Times* declared that: 'The wreck (of the *Earl of Chester*) is now a prey to the notorious wreckers of the coast known to Welsh seafaring men as Lladron Crigyll (*the Crigyll robbers*). Many hundreds of them were there yesterday stealing whatever they could carry away.'

The original 'gang', though, was active as early as 1715, when in fact its members were brought to trial, It is on record that: 'On Tuesday 25 April, 1715, at the County Gaol, Beaumaris, were committed for felony three men, known as the Lladron Creigiau Crigyll (*the robbers of Crigyll rocks*), who were found guilty of plundering the wreck of the sloop called *The Charming Jenny* stranded at Crigyll.'

Those were days of harsh punishments, when even the theft of a loaf of bread was a hanging offence, and it is very probable that this little band of wreckers met with a sad though not undeserved end. Another writer of roughly the same period noted of a different wreck: '. . . the owner. . . is come hear, and is going to hang half a dozen of the Thieves who rob'd the wreck'.

Another band of Crigyll wreckers — Owen John Ambrose of Llanfihangel-yn-Nhywyn, Gabriel Roberts of Ceirchiog, Thomas Roberts of Llanfaelog and Hugh Griffith Hughes, also of Llanfaelog — were more fortunate. They were tried in April, 1741, at Beaumaris Assizes, before Mr Justice Martyn. All were accused of robbing a Liverpool brigantine, the *Loveday & Betty*, which had been driven onshore and stranded by the south-westerly gales of 31 December, 1740. Once again, the penalty they faced for felony was the noose, and the trial attracted such a lot of attention that many notable businessmen travelled to Beaumaris to attend it.

One of these, William Bulkeley, recorded in his diary: 'Tho this is the last day of the Sessions the Court sat to try causes till 3 in the

Evening; a thing never known before in the history of man. Martyn the Judge being every day drunk deferred all business to the last, when they were hustled over in a very unbecoming manner.'

Much to the horror of everyone, including a gentleman called Lewis Morris (father of William Morris, whose 'Plans of Harbours' has already been referred to, and who had for several years been himself a customs officer at Holyhead and Beaumaris) Judge Martyn remained in such a drunken state that he discharged all the prisoners, notwithstanding the fact that they were obviously guilty. In a poem which was to become a popular ballad everywhere, Lewis Morris passionately declaimed against their freedom and spoke of the hanging he insisted they had deserved. The following extract gives us some idea of how strongly the people of the coast felt about the unholy deeds of the wreckers:

> 'How fine to the good and honest
> Is the light of candle and fire;
> How fine to the brigands of the night
> Is to be in darkened houses;
> How fine to my ears is it to hear
> Of the hanging of the Thieves of Crigyll.
>
> It is a village without the fear of God,
> Where evil lives in the hearts of men,
> Bandits of the waves, vicious villains
> Hiding their lanterns under their cloaks;
> May God keep innocent travellers
> From wrecking on the rocks of Crigyll.'

Less villainous, possibly, but responsible for much of the activity round the coast especially on dark nights, were the gangs of smugglers, who often included whole communities. They flourished pretty well unhindered until the creation of the coastguard in 1822 signalled a clamp-down by the government on their activities.

One of the most notorious smuggling gangs of Wales was the Lucas family of Stout Hall, Glamorgan. One of the early sons of the family, John Lucas, a lawless young man who, so we are told, combined a handsome exterior with a violent temper, was given by his father 'a residence at Porth Einon called "Ye Salte House" ', and this he proceed to establish as the headquarters for his nefarious activities.

He apparently set to 'storing said stronghold with arms and also rebuilded and repaired another stronghold called Kulverd Hall near thereto in the rocks and rendered both inaccessible save for passage thereunto through the clift. . . He became outlaw, engaged in smuggling matters "secoured ye pirates and ye French smugglers and rifled ye wrecked ships and forced mariners to serve him".'

The reign of the Lucas family lasted nearly 200 years, ending when the occupant of Salt House, another John Lucas, died in 1703 and the house was left empty. The whole family had followed, to varying extents, in the footsteps of the early John Lucas as smugglers. The cellars of the house were so huge that it was possible to drive a horse and cart into them, and it was rumoured after John Lucas' death that the last 'run' of French wines and silks had not had time to be distributed, and was still hidden somewhere within these cellars. But in spite of much energetic investigating by would-be treasure seekers, the treasure was never found — or if it was, the finders gave nothing away.

Chapter Six

Phantoms from the Wreck

It is not a common occurrence for the victims of a wreck to come back and haunt the more fortunate living. But it was reported in no less reputable a newspaper than the *Daily Mirror* on Wednesday, October 10th, 1990, that villagers near the scene of the most dreadful wreck ever to occur in Rhosili Bay, on the Gower, were being haunted by drowned victims from their watery grave.

The ship in question was a small paddle-steamer, the *City of Bristol* which was returning home from Waterford on the night of November 17th-18th, 1840, when a terrible gale drove her off course, and she ended up going aground just north of Diles Lake, after making efforts to reach shelter in Rhosili Bay.

Once aground, she turned in the heavy seas and was pounded without mercy by the breakers. The crew hoped that she would float on the flood tide, and the seas were too rough to do anything but pray — however, prayers were in vain, and just after midnight, the *City of Bristol* broke in two, and her crew and cargo were thrown to the maw of the breakers.

What seems so tragic about this wreck was that it was a homely sort of vessel. Apart from a crew of 17, there were 7 passengers on board, of whom two were women and one a child. Also, as was common on Irish packet boats, large numbers of livestock were travelling in pens on the deck. When the ship broke up, a total of 100 pigs and 18 cattle as well as 600 sacks of oats, disappeared along with the crew and passengers into the thundering blackness of the seas.

Only two men and a few of the livestock survived. One cattleman clung grimly to the tail of a bullock as it scrambled for the shore, and was able to reach it in safety. The other man to escape was the ship's carpenter. All the rest met their fate in the dark swirling waters.

Over the years, the remains of the wreck have sometimes been able to be seen if the sands — those terrible drifting, shifting sands we have already come across in the story of the "Dollar Ship" — had moved with the tide to reveal them. But nobody ever reported that the ghosts of the dead from the *City of Bristol* had crept from the wreck to move across the sands and hunt out the living.

In October 1990, however, storms once again uncovered the wreck, and the reports of the villagers were that spectral hands — the small hands of the women and the little one of the dead baby, as well as those of the men — were tapping on their windows and keeping them from their sleep. Incredible? Possibly — but would *you* like to keep watch on a dark night to see whether the sad procession of sea-weed-shrouded sailors and the two unfortunate women, the child walking beside them, emerge to make their way inland on their grisly errand?

Chapter Seven
Disasters at Sea

The legal definition of a ship that is wrecked is not, as we might imagine, that the vessel has to be cast up on a shore where it is battered to pieces, or run aground. Any ship which is lost, for whatever reason, whether run aground, cast up on the shore, broken by rocks or even caused to sink because of accidents such as fire, for instance is actually 'wrecked' if the ship herself is lost.

Thus wrecks do not always take place on or near the shore, and ships can be wrecked while at sea, or even in harbour. And there are a large number of things that can go wrong in order to cause the wreck.

Amazingly enough, a very large percentage of ships are wrecked through collision. It is difficult to believe that with all the wide expanse of sea where they can sail, large numbers of them accidentally collide with each other. This has always been the case, and one might have thought that with all the technical developments which have made sailing a ship so much easier than the hit and miss techniques of the past, such accidents would decrease as the years go by.

In fact, the opposite has happened. In about 1979, it was estimated that there were over 150 collisions occurring every month in some part of the world, and the numbers were not becoming reduced. The most notorious region for collisions was then — and probably still is — the Straits of Dover, where at that time 750 ships used the area every day.

Even though the task of the seaman was made easier by the

introduction of radar, ship-to-shore communications and other technical aids, the fact that there were more and more ships to make use of the shipping lanes meant that there was a greater chance that there might be a collision. And when steamships were involved rather than just the old sailing vessels, the dangers increased, for since the steamships could go faster than sail, they would, if they hit another vessel, have a much harder impact and could do more damage.

But even in the days of the sailing ships, terrible collisions could and did occur, and the waters off the Welsh coasts saw their share of tragedy.

The waters off Holyhead have been the scene of many dreadful collisions. The first to be recorded took place on February 20th, 1841, though there had undoubtedly been innumerable such disasters in the past. On this occasion, the American sailing ship *Governor Fenner*, was en route from Liverpool to New York, carrying a cargo of iron, when she collided in thick fog with the paddle steamer *Nottingham*. The impact must have been horrific, for the bows of the *Governor Fenner* were smashed and she sank. 123 lives were lost, these being mostly emigrants on their way to make a new life in the United States, but destined never to reach New York.

The paddle steamer, which was carrying cattle and sheep, was badly damaged, but managed to dock safely. There does not seem to have been loss of life here, though there appears to be no record of what happened to the animals, and whether they survived the tragedy.

Some forty years later, however, on the Irish Sea route between Holyhead and Dublin, another tragic collision occurred where the animal travellers were not so fortunate. This did not happen in fog but during the black hours of the night — at midnight, October 31st, 1883. It involved the German sailing barque *Alhambra* and the London and North Western Railway's cattle steamship *Holyhead*, which was packed with cattle. As a result of the collision, both of these ships were lost. They sank, taking fifteen men — as well as all the cattle — with them.

Yet another tragedy which might have been almost humorous if it had not been so pitiful, happened on January 7th, 1843 when the wooden paddle-steamer *Monk* was travelling from Porthdinllaen to Liverpool. The captain, whose name was Hughes, had allowed the vessel to be heavily overloaded before she sailed, and she was not only leaking but filled to overflowing with 140 pigs and £600 worth of

Welsh butter, when she set out. In addition, there were the eighteen owners of the pigs and butter, as well as eight members of the crew also crammed on board.

It was not dark night, but the light was failing when Captain Hughes attempted to negotiate the dangerous Caernarfon Bar. A combination of failing light, ebbing tide and faulty steering gear caused the vessel to strike the North Bank, and those on board did what they could to try and escape.

Three of the passengers and the engineer managed to reach safety in the ship's punt, and they notified the Llanddwyn lifeboat, which was able to take two more survivors from the bows of the stricken ship, but the other nineteen men were never found. The captain, he who had been the cause of the whole tragedy through his careless overloading of the vessel and his irresponsible attempt to get past the Caernarfon Bar when it was not safe to do so, was washed ashore at Belan. Sadly, his corpse was accompanied by many corpses of most of the 140 pigs which had been travelling with him!

The worst time for collisions would seem to be in the dark hours and in foggy weather. Another collision which took place in thick fog, happened on August 8th, 1901, in the St George's Channel between Wales and Ireland. Off the dreaded Tuskar Rock, the steamship *Kincora*, which was bound from Limerick to Liverpool, was cautiously groping her way. She had reduced speed, and was sounding her fog horn, though she had no idea that any other vessel was in the vicinity. All of a sudden, as though from no-where, a huge bulk loomed out of the fog above her. It was the White Star liner *Oceanic*, which, unable to stop itself, ran her down.

It took only the space of seven minutes after she had been hit, that the *Kincora* had sunk into the depths — with the tragic loss of seven lives.

Many of the ships which came to grief off the Welsh coast were filled — as was the *Governor Fenner* — with emigrants, mostly Irish, who embarked from Liverpool for a new life in the United States. Crossings of the Atlantic by steamer had been made early on in the nineteenth century — taking twenty-eight days — but it was round about the middle of the century that regular crossings to transport mail and passengers from Britain to America were established, the first contract going to Samuel Cunard whose *Britannia* left Liverpool on July 4th, 1840, its owners the British & North American Royal Mail Steam Packet Co.

From then on, Liverpool was recognised as the gateway to America. It was from here that the thousands of emigrants embarked in their search for a new and better life. The conditions under which they sailed were hardly luxurious at the best of times, and on occasion could be horrific. For instance, when Welsh slates were shipped aboard as cargo, their weight in relation to their bulk left quite lot of empty space in the holds. Many of the emigrants paid in order to travel alongside the slates in these empty spaces!

Warnings about the inadvisability of taking this course of action, such as when a young Welshman called Dafydd Shone Harry wrote home from America to his family in Merioneth in 1817: 'If any of you are for coming here, take care not to come with slates from Caernarfon', failed to put the eager emigrants off.

Typical of this period, and telling us a great deal about what it was like to travel as an emigrant, are the details on a poster currently in Caernarfon public library. This advertises:

'For New York, Direct.
The fine fast sailing barque *Hindoo*, of Caernarfon, burthen about 600 tons (The sole property of Mr H. Owen, Rhyddgar, Anglesey), Richard Hughes, Commander, will be ready to sail from this port on or about the middle of March next with a ballast of slates. Emigrants will find this conveyance most convenient for embarking for the United States, the vessel being properly fitted out for the accommodation of passengers. For freight and passage, and further particulars, an early application is required to be made to the Commander on board, or to John Owen, High Street.
Caernarfon.
1st Feb 1843.'

This sounds luxurious in the extreme, but in fact, the accommodation which the ship provided for passengers, and the 'fitting out' with this in mind, simply meant that when the slates were stowed, they were stacked so that there were gaps between the piles of slate, which the wretched emigrants could occupy. They not only had to pay £10 for each family for this privilege, they also had to provide their own food and bedding! All the ship offered to help them endure a journey that might confine them in their tiny little space between the slates for anything up to ten weeks, was water and fuel.

But the emigrants did set out with hearts high with hope, dreaming of a glowing future. Sadly, however, many of them never reached the land where their new lives were waiting.

On August 24th, 1848, for instance, the *Ocean Monarch*, a full-rigged American ship of 1500 tons, set sail from Liverpool to Boston. Apart from a crew of 42, she was carrying 354 passengers, most of them Irish emigrants en route to find their fortune and their crock of gold at the end of the rainbow.

Just off the Welsh coast near Colwyn Bay, fire broke out. The captain reported: 'We were then about six miles east of the Great Orme . . . The steward of the ship came up and told me that one of the passengers had lit a fire in one of the ventilators in the afterpart of the ship. . .' (one cannot help but wonder if this passenger was slightly deranged, if he did indeed do such a senseless thing) '. . . I at once went below and discovered smoke proceeding into the main cabin, through one of the state-rooms. We began without delay to throw water down; but in five minutes afterwards, indeed almost instantly, the after part of the ship burst into flames.'

The story was later changed, and the cause of the fire variously given as the pipe smoking of the steerage passengers, or one of the crew carelessly taking a candle into a store containing straw and spirits. What is certain is that the fire was very soon out of control, raging unchecked throughout the vessel. The flames lit up the whole area, and were visible from all along the coast, causing several other vessels to go to the stricken ship's aid.

Those which arrived to render assistance were the *Queen of the Ocean*, which was owned by the Commodore of the Royal Mersey Yacht Club; the Brazilian navy steam frigate *Affonso*, the City of Dublin Steam Packet Co paddler *Prince of Wales* and the *New World*, a packet ship outward bound to New York.

The Commodore of the Yacht Club, who was on his way home from Beaumaris regatta, got there first and was able to pick up thirty-two survivors. The *Affonso* rescued 156, and the other vessels rendered sterling assistance, but in spite of their efforts, 178 of the emigrants died, while the *Ocean Monarch* burned for twenty-four hours and at last sank on the afternoon of August 25th.

At Porth Newry in Caernarfon Bay, yet another emigrant ship came to a sad end. This was the 500 ton vessel *Newry*, (after which Porth Newry was named). She was two days out from Warren Point, County

Down, carrying 400 emigrants who were bound for Quebec. Early on the morning of April 16th, 1830, the ship was wrecked.

An eye-witness account tells us that:

'At the time the vessel struck the passengers were all in their berths, and most of them seasick. Upon perceiving their danger a dreadful scene of terror and confusion arose. Nearly all of them rushed upon deck with no other clothing except that in which they had lain down for the night.'

The captain, in an effort to bridge the gap between the stranded ship and the shore, gave orders that the main mast should be cut down, which was done. The idea was of course so that the passengers could be assisted to escape from ship to shore across the gap of the waves, by means of this 'bridge', but in fact as soon as the mast was down, practically the whole crew except for the mate and a seaman whose name was Hale, immediately disappeared into the darkness, their only thought to save their own skins.

But there were still heroes about, even though the crew of Captain Crosby had proved to be so cowardly. A local sailor, David Griffiths of Plas Bodafon, boarded the wrecked vessel using the same mast by which the crew had escaped. For ten hours, he and three other local men — Owen James, Richard Griffiths and John Pritchard — worked with the captain, the mate and seaman Hale to try and get the passengers off the ship. By means of ropes, and using the mast as a bridge, 375 men, women and children were saved from the terrors of the wreck.

But even though passengers might have escaped from a wreck and been saved from the jaws of death, this was not the end of their trials in the days before there were fast ambulance services to whisk survivors off to hospital. As historian Ivor Wynne Jones informs us:

'After the terror of a night-time scramble into the unknown or the horror of a daylight crossing of the chasm containing the bodies of some of the twenty-five who had fallen during the night, the survivors were faced with a 60-mile walk to Holyhead wearing little or no clothing and no shoes. Most of the emigrants arrived at Caernarfon on Sunday, 18 April — the day on which the *Newry* broke up — without any of their meagre possessions having been salvaged. After a meal and four shillings (20p) each out of a fund collected by Deputy Mayor William Roberts, they went on their way, sharing a further £37 collected at Bangor on the Monday. It was Friday before they left

Holyhead aboard two Liverpool steamers, the *Satellite* and the *Abbey*.'

David Griffiths, the man who had organised the rescue and worked so hard to save the survivors, was awarded the Silver Medal of the RNLI for his gallantry, as well as £10 from Lloyds and £10 from the Underwriters' Committee of Liverpool.

As a last comment on the many other disasters which happened to emigrant ships, we can cite the cases of the *Fomalhaut* and the *Lady Louisa Pennant*, both of which were Bangor-built schooners. They left Port Penrhyn, carrying cargoes of slate, on October 14th, 1902, and neither was heard of again. It was thought that they had collided with each other — and we can only hope that there were no little huddled families of emigrants trying to make themselves at home between the piles of slate in the holds!

In the next chapter, we shall be hearing more about ships which sailed out of harbour — only to vanish.

Chapter Eight
Into Thin Air

Wales has had its own great mysteries of the sea to rival the *Mary Celeste*, where the vessel was found drifting with not a soul on board, even though mugs of tea were only half drank and still steaming hot. What had happened to the crew? No-one has ever been able to give the answer.

Not quite so well-known is the tale of the *Pacific*, a wooden paddle-steamer which had already made a name for herself in May, 1851, when she set a new record for crossing the Atlantic. She made the journey in nine days, twenty hours and ten minutes.

In the January of 1856, however, the *Pacific* set quite a different sort of record. The 2860 ton vessel left Liverpool for New York, her last sight of land probably being the Anglesey coast before she disappeared — into thin air. Nothing was ever heard of her again. No messages were received, and there was no trace of wreckage, corpses or any clue that she had existed at all.

She quite simply vanished, and so did all the 186 people who were aboard. They probably imagined — in view of the vessel's record — that they would have a speedy passage, but little did those who boarded her at Liverpool, before setting out past the North Wales coast, realise that their journey was indeed to be quicker than they expected, and not to the destination they were hopefully anticipating.

There were always the strongest links between the seamen of Wales

— ship-owners and ship-builders as well as the sailors and those who 'went down to the sea in ships' — and the ship-brokers of Liverpool, many of whom were themselves Welsh.

In the 1870s, a former pupil teacher from Llanrhuddlad, William Thomas, had become well established as a ship-broker in Liverpool, running a company with many vessels. He wrote that he had 'bought the following ships for myself and other friends as Co-owners, and have had the sole control and management of them since, viz. in the year 1872, *North Star, Lady Young,* 1873 *Sappho,* 1874 *Malabar, Julia,* 1875 *Buckhorn* and *Havelock.*'

These were only a few of the ships owned and managed by William Thomas, Llanrhuddlad and Liverpool, and it is amazing how many of the list — probably typical of the lists of other owners at that time too — met some sort of mysterious end.

The *Lady Young* was lost in 1880, though this does not appear to have been a mystery and her loss was recorded 'between Plymouth and the Start on her way to Cardiff'. The *Malabar* is starkly recorded as 'Missing 1888', with no suggestion as to where or how.

But the *Julia* and the *Buckhorn* are almost as mysterious as the elusive *Pacific*. The *Julia* was bound from New York to Liverpool with a cargo of rosin and petroleum, with a crew of 12, and she was last heard of on September 2nd, 1874, presumably when she left New York. After that — nothing, and it was assumed that her crew had drowned.

The same thing happened to the *Buckhorn*, which was travelling from St Helena en route to England, with a cargo of 1,147 tons of rice. After leaving St Helena on November 8th, 1876, the vessel sailed into obscurity, never to be seen or heard of again, and once more the crew — of 16 this time — were presumed drowned.

There were other ships owned by William Thomas which simply disappeared. In January, 1880, on route from Astoria to Queenstown with a cargo of wheat, the *County of Denbigh* took a crew of 20 with it; and in 1895, the *Menai* left Newcastle, New South Wales, its destination Tocopilla. Once it had sailed out of the harbour, however, it was never seen or heard of again — and needless to say, neither it nor any members of its crew ever reached Tocopilla.

The *Principality* was last spoken to on the 13th July, 1905, when its course was from Junin to Rotterdam, its cargo nitrates of soda.

Afterwards, nothing, and once more the crew of 25 was supposed drowned.

The *Nation* was assumed to have been lost in a hurricane. The vessel was not heard of after leaving Rangoon in March, 1892, but it was calculated that the ship probably encountered a hurricane then off Mauritius, and this was what caused the deaths of the 30-strong crew.

Sometimes it was possible to assume that bad weather or some other catastrophe known to be in the vicinity where a ship was likely to be at that time, had caused the tragedy but in many cases, the disappearance of the vessel remained a complete mystery.

Another William Thomas vessel to go down — or go somewhere — mysteriously was the *Dominion*, which was never heard of after leaving Honolulu for Royal Roads, British Columbia, on 19 January, 1899. And the *Annie Thomas* was last spoken to on 19th October, 1899, on a voyage from Cardiff to Acapulco with a cargo of coal. She too mysteriously vanished, along with her crew of 27.

So even as the century was turning into a new age of scientific achievement and technology, it was still possible for a ship to sail out of harbour into nowhere. These were not just sailors' stories — they were recorded happenings — and as we have seen, mysterious disappearances happened to Welsh ships as well as those of other nationalities.

But before we become too carried away by the spooky thrill of it all, let's hear what one expert on Welsh sea-faring has to say about the subject. Speaking of the *Menai*, the historian Aled Eames comments: '. . . she disappeared without trace, possibly another victim of the careless coal trimmers of Newcastle. Shifting cargoes killed many ships.'

But not all those which disappeared, surely!

Chapter Nine
Great Escapes

Among the many wrecks which have taken place around the coasts of Wales, what strikes the observer so often is not whether the ship or its crew was lost or saved, but the amazing way in which the rescue happened.

Take, for instance, the case of the 280-ton Liverpool brig *Hornby*, which was caught in a terrible storm when outward bound to Rio de Janeiro and was held up for several days between Orme's Head and Lynas. On New Year's Day, 1824, she was very close to the rocks under the Great Orme, and was rolling wildly. Within minutes, she had foundered and the fifteen people on board her — twelve crew members and two passengers — were lost.

There was one incredible exception, however. As the ship had rolled, her masts practically touching the cliffs, one seaman called John Williams happened to be aloft in the rigging, since he had been ordered to loose the jib. He suddenly found himself level with a ledge or rock on the cliff, and without pausing to think, he leaped to safety.

A contemporary account written by the MP Thomas Peers Williams of Craig-y-don, continues:

'When he recovered himself he saw no more of the ship and, the next morning, he clambered up the precipice and told the story.'

In fact, his ship and those aboard had gone down soon after his fateful leap. But he doggedly climbed from his solitary ledge, handhold by handhold, up the cliffs and eventually reached a part of the old coppermine workings where the miners hard at work were staggered by his sudden appearance from no-where. He must have found himself at home among the miners, for he never ventured to sea again, prefering to spend the rest of his life as a miner himself in Llandudno. It is related that in his old age, he lived very well off the handouts of tourists who were thrilled to hear the tale of his escape from his own lips as a genuine survivor of a genuine shipwreck.

On August 28th, 1831, the *Burmese*, en route from St Petersburg carrying a cargo of tallow, became stranded not far from Point of Ayr. On this occasion, it was not so much a question of saving the crew — and the master's wife, who was also aboard — but of granting them permission to be rescued. As a precaution against cholera, none of the seventeen members of the crew, nor the master and his wife, were allowed to leave the ship for the shore for what must have seemed to them like an eternity, but was in fact four hours.

While they were waiting, the master's wife was lashed to the deck for safety, since huge seas were breaking right over the vessel. We can imagine how they felt when at long last, they were allowed ashore. Even the fact that they had to spend the next several days in quarantine could not have dimmed for the survivors the fact that they were, actually, alive and that they had survived.

Often, the circumstances of the rescue called for initiative and the use of whoever — or whatever — was to hand. On July 29th, 1835, the smack *Active*, anchored in Ramsey Bay, Isle of Man, began to drag her anchors in the teeth of a strong north-westerly gale. She quickly drifted out to sea, and in the end went aground in Cemaes Bay, Anglesey, but quite a long way from the shore.

Various attempts were made to launch a boat, but in the end, the five members of the crew, who were huddled exhausted below decks, were spectacularly rescued by none other than a clergyman. A clergyman — and a horse.

The Rev. James Williams, realising the urgency of the situation, galloped on horseback into the surf to try and get near enough to be able to throw a grappling hook and line to the wrecked ship. Clinging to his horse, half-riding, half-swimming, he managed to get the hook over the bowsprit, and as a result, five lives were saved.

For risking his own life in this very brave and gallant action, the

Rev. Williams received the first Gold Medal of the RNLI which was ever awarded to Wales.

Another instance when much-coveted RNLI medals were earned by the rescuers, who displayed dedication and gallantry far beyond the ordinary call of duty, happened a few miles to the north of Point Lynas on October 28th, 1927. The ketch *Excel* was in difficulties and waterlogged in the teeth of a gale, and she had been taken in tow by a German freighter, but on the arrival on the scene of the Moelfre lifeboat *Charles and Eliza Laura*, the freighter cut her adrift.

She was already sinking, but after some consultation between the Coxwain and one of the crew, Captain Owen Jones, the lifeboat actually sailed over the sunken bows of the ketch and managed to snatch the three-man crew, who were clinging to the rigging, to safety. In the course of this desperate rescue, however, the hull of the lifeboat was shattered and she was unable to return to Moelfre.

For thirteen hours, almost sinking but for their air cases, the crew battled with the waves and with their own exhaustion and shock. They managed to anchor off Puffin Island, where the motor lifeboat from Beaumaris came to their rescue. But during that ghastly night, one of the survivors from the *Excel* and a member of the lifeboat's crew both died.

All in all, this was a spectacular rescue, and it comes as no surprise to hear that the Coxwain and Captain Owen Jones, a master mariner who had sat in for a member of the regular crew who was ill, received Gold Medals. All the rest of the crew were awarded Bronze Medals. The gallant little lifeboat *Charles and Eliza Laura* had, however, been damaged beyond repair and was replaced.

A rather less creditable episode concerning a lifeboat happened in 1851, when the Shipwrecked Fishermen & Mariners' Benevolent Society were beginning to provide lifeboat stations. One of them was for Porthmadog, and the crew might well have been looking forward to something very special, as the boats had been built to the design which had received the prize in the Duke of Northumberland's competition held in that year.

The Porthmadog boat was delivered to Caernarfon and the proud crew went along to collect her. It was fortunate that no immediate wreck required assistance, for the new boat did not even make it back to Porthmadog. She capsized in the Menai Straits and the crew had to be rescued themselves by the Caernarfon No. 2 lifeboat, and a boat from a schooner which happened to be in the vicinity.

The new lifeboat was ignominiously towed all the way back to the harbour, upside down. Two of her air cases were filled with water, and it took several months for the necessary repairs to be completed.

An unusual escape occurred aboard the brig *Sapho* in 1839, when a westerly gale drove her into Caernarfon Bay. Captain Wallace, the master, was obviously not an optimistic sort of person, for he gathered the crew together and presented each man with two sovereigns, with orders that these should be sewn into a safe pocket, as they were to pay for the men's burial the next day.

In fact, his pessimistic expectation that the ship and her crew were about to come to grief was quite justified. A funeral was duly arranged for Captain Wallace and six of his crew, who were laid to rest at Nefyn in a common grave. But the man who arranged it was the one person who had survived the catastrophe — an apprentice. The ship had been bound for Liverpool carrying a cargo of treacle from the West Indies, and when the worst of the tragedy was over, the apprentice was discovered safe and sound on the beach, having sought safety in an empty treacle barrel!

Anything can be expected in the case of a wreck. Sometimes the ships themselves take it into their heads to act in a most unpredictable manner. In the case of the *William Carey*, en route from Calcutta to Liverpool, she had hit the Caernarfon Bar on February 12th, 1856, and was obviously in difficulties when the Llanddwyn lifeboat came to her aid and began to save the crew. They had taken off nineteen men and only the master, the mate and one seaman were still on board when the *William Carey* suddenly decided to refloat.

She began to drift away from the lifeboat, and in epic manner, one of the Llanddwyn crew who was also a Caernarfon Bar pilot seized a rope and swung on board. With her new crew of four, the ship was sailed into Caernarfon, and in the long run did complete her voyage to Liverpool. So this was one case where the ship turned into a survivor rather than the people aboard her.

Animals came to the rescue once again with regard to the brig *Athena*, whose hulk, lost among the sands of Malltraeth beach is referred to locally as '*y llong Groeg*' or 'the Greek ship'. Candia-based, she was on her way to Liverpool carrying a cargo of beans from Alexandria when on December 20th, 1852, she was wrecked on the sands. The local people made several attempts to pull their lifeboat round the southern tip of Llanddwyn with no success, and then took the inspired action of bringing in a team of horses from Newborough.

With the horses gamely tugging the 18 cwt boat, the men were able to cross the dunes to launch their vessel much closer to the wrecked *Athena*. Fourteen men were saved on this occasion, and the Llanddwyn pilots displayed a similar enterprise when they saved nine men on December 26th and thirteen on 27th. They were rewarded for this last by the RNLI thanks on vellum for the coxwain, Hugh Williams.

Yet another miraculous escape happened to the crew of the *Southern Cross*, a Liverpool ship built for the Australia run. On March 15th, 1855, she was sailing from London when she hit a rock off Rhoscolyn Head. It was not long before she sank, but in the meantime the whole crew of seventeen had managed to escape in the ship's boat.

It was dark and there was a mist, so we can imagine the plight of these ship-wrecked mariners. In their inability to see where they were drifting, they went straight into another rock and the ship's boat wrecked them for a second time. Fortunately the rock was just big enough for them to be able to cluster on it, sitting or lying, but they must have been extremely uncomfortable for it was a full twelve hours before anyone noticed their situation. Even then, they had to wait for Rhoscolyn lifeboat to make two perilous trips to pick them up, through dangerous rocky waters. But at least they had survived being ship-wrecked not just once, but twice!

The crew of the 855-ton clipper *Norman Court* achieved an incredible escape from their vessel when she was returning from Java with a cargo of sugar, and went aground on the Crigyll rocks, tearing out her bottom. Her captain, Captain McBride, was later blamed for faulty navigation which caused the accident. It was indeed dreadful for the ship's mainmast collapsed and smashed the ship's boats. Her crew were visible when day dawned, clinging in desperation to the rigging.

Attempts were made to fire a rocket with a line from the shore, but five times, in the strong wind blowing, the line fell short, and although the lifeboat at Rhoscolyn might have been able to reach the ship and rescue the survivors, she had been damaged a few days before and was beached in Trearddur Bay.

The lifeboat at Rhosneigr was the next choice, even though she would be heading into the wind and would have to pass through two bad reefs to reach the *Norman Court*, and she gallantly ventured into the waves. She had almost managed to get to the stricken vessel when she was thrown on her beam ends. In the confusion, one member of the crew was actually tossed out, but managed to save himself by seizing one of the lifelines.

Eventually, in a state of exhaustion, the crew of the lifeboat, with nothing accomplished, returned to Rhosneigr, and even though they tried again in the afternoon, they once more were forced to turn back. Still the survivors from the *Norman Court* were desperately clinging to the rigging, but they had been there since some time the previous night, and must have been failing both mentally as well as physically, having seen rescue so close at hand, only to be snatched, as it were, from their grasp.

Obviously some more drastic action was called for. It was now dark, and the men of Rhosneigr were reluctant to make a third attempt to try and reach the *Norman Court*. So the secretary of the Rhoscolyn lifeboat made an appeal to Holyhead, as a result of which the Holyhead lifeboat crew were dramatically hurried by a special train to Rhosneigr. They proceeded to launch the local boat, and succeeded in rescuing the twenty survivors who were still hanging onto the rigging of the doomed ship. We can imagine how very glad those tired men were to see them!

This gallant effort resulted in a RNLI Silver Medal for the Coxwain, Edward Jones.

Two odd cargoes which were 'saved' with immense enthusiasm by the local people came ashore at Overton Mere and Paviland Cliff, in South Wales. The wreck at Overton took place in 1865 of the schooner *Frances & Ann*, which on January 26th of that year was driven ashore on the pebble beach in very heavy seas and winds of gale force. As she broke up, her whole cargo of oranges scattered far and wide, turning the beach into a gigantic fruit stall of which the local people were quick to take advantage. It is little wonder that this wreck was referred to afterwards as the "Orange Vessel".

Rather less colourful, but just as useful so far as the locals were concerned, was the more recent wreck of the *Ben Blanche* in 1933. The *Ben Blanche*, with a cargo of potatoes, was driven ashore in thick fog under Paviland Cliff on an exceptionally dark night. When the Rhosili rocket crew arrived and got a line aboard her, they discovered when dawn came that the crew had already left the wreck and been picked up by another vessel. The wreck herself was a total loss — but we can be sure that large numbers of eager 'rescuers' made sure the potato cargo did not go to waste!

Another odd piece of 'salvage' accompanied the grounding of the 2,500 ton steamship *Epidauro*, which came to grief at Overton Cliffs on Feburary 13th, 1913. When some of the crew managed to get ashore in their ship's boat, the Port Einon lifeboat was launched and saved three of these crew members who, on returning to the ship, were thrown into the sea as their boat capsized. Heroics were not necessary, as once the tide ebbed, the vessel was left stranded, so that the shocked and frightened crew were able to get ashore.

The ship was a total wreck, but amongst items which were to be salvaged was her boiler, and a local man was employed to climb inside and fit 400 wooden plugs. This took him several days, but at last he had finished and made to climb out of the boiler for the last time. What horror when he stuck fast, and had to be cut out of the manhole!

It is recorded that another local man advised those around to: 'Say thee prayers boys, for Davey Jones'll have 'ee 'fore ever Old Nick, he getteth you into the bathing drawers.' As a fitting finale to this tale of melodrama, the boiler when eventually moved was towed only 200 yards before it sank. The hapless owners, washing their hands of the troublesome thing, promptly abandoned it — so there it lies still.

Another variation of the 'salvage' theme happened in 1881 when the *Cresswell* went ashore under Paviland Cliffs and the coastguard, on arriving at the scene of the wreck, found that some of the crew were still on board and called out the Rhosili rocket crew. They soon had a line out to the vessel, and each member of the crew took his place in the breeches buoy and was hauled ashore.

The last man, however, caused them quite a lot of trouble. First of all, he could not get intò the chair; and once he had been brought ashore, he could not get out again. As he was being assisted to struggle free, he began to curse the coastguard and complain about the rough ride he had had. Then to the astonishment of all, he proceeded to take off his clothes. First his suit — under which he had a second suit — and beneath that, a third! Little wonder that he had found climbing into the breeches buoy and out of it difficult, wearing, as he had been, three complete suits of clothes. He had been one survivor who had certainly seen to it that he survived complete with a full wardrobe!

At an earlier period, one of the strangest cargoes that must surely ever have been 'saved' off the Welsh coast belonged to a ship called the *Shepton Mallet* which on February 15th, 1731 was 'lost near Worms Head'. This was one of the first recorded wrecks on the Gower, and the records inform us that the vessel was 'of and for Bristol, William Hellier Master'. She was sailing from Barbados 'having on board 72 hogs heads of sugar, 19 tierces, 19 barrels and 1 bagge of cotton and 204 elephants teeth.'

Apparently the authorities were only driven to record this particular wreck because of the shocking activities of the local people. When listing the cargo, particularly the elephants' tusks, the customs officer who was making the report added: '. . . some small part of which has been carried off by ye country, 51 of ye teeth are saved and secured under the Kings lock. The master and 5 men are saved.'

But before the customs officers had even heard about the wreck, the country people had had several days to help themselves in a leisurely manner to whatever they wanted, and when three officers arrived on the scene to recover the cargo, they found precious little, only a few of the 'teeth' mentioned.

The disappearance of the cargo was considered so severe a crime that the authorities did not give up even when their searches failed to bring any more of the missing objects to light. Zealously, they posted up the following over a wide area covering twenty parishes:

'This is to give notice to all persons concerned in taking away, concealing or receiving any of the elephants' teeth, cotton or other goods salved out of ye Shepton Mallet of Bristol, lately stranded near Porteinon, and if they do not bring forthwith the goods to ye Customs Ho. Wareho or Mr Caleb Thomas' at Pitten, they will be prosecuted as ye law directs.'

A few more tusks were handed in but as for the most part, those six-foot long pieces of ivory had vanished apparently into thin air. We cannot help but wonder where they went to, exactly, for they would have been rather difficult to hide, and of precious little use, one would imagine, to the local peasantry. But no doubt the Welsh, shrewd as always, found some way of disposing of them at a profit to themselves, and lived for months off their exotic harvest from this particular wreck.

Rather less exotic was the survivor of the French Schooner *Surprise* when she was driven ashore under Overton Cliffs on a storm-tossed night in February of 1883. Between the sharp fangs of the rocks and the fury of the sea which threw them to their fate against those same black instruments of oblivion, the crew of seven vanished to be either drowned or battered to death. Their mutilated bodies were washed ashore — but one member of the ship's company who not only managed to scramble determinedly ashore but who was responsible for alerting local attention to the fact that there had been a wreck was a black retriever. Very wet, very tired, very bewildered — but out of all the living creatures who had been on that vessel, the only one still alive.

A hilarious 'rescue' took place during one of the occasions when the Port Einon lifeboat *Janet* was called out during her ten years of service. It was a foggy day, and the boat was launched to go to the assistance of a vessel in difficulties below Paviland. Grimly and gallantly, the crew toiled at their oars, ploughing onwards and yet ever onwards through the murk of the fog, yet never reaching their objective.

When at length the fog lifted somewhat, the reason why it was taking them so long to hurry to the rescue became obvious. The Deputy Coxwain had absentmindedly neglected to pull the pin from the compass, which had consequently remained fixed, so that the crew had been going determinedly round — in circles! They were still in Port Einon Bay.

Once this little slip had been brought to their notice, however, it was not long before they were on the scene where they were needed and able to give the necessary assistance — though it was a long time before the Deputy Coxwain stopped being referred to as 'Compass Bill' by his comrades.

Even more nonchalant was the escape of the crew from the *Pass of Balmaha* of Glasgow, which was sheltering from the gales off Moelfre on December 28th, 1900. She sent a distress call as her anchors were dragging, and twenty-six of her crew were taken off by a lifeboat. However, when they were safe, a roll-call revealed that there were two men missing, so the lifeboat turned round and headed for the wreck again. Lo and behold, the two missing crew members were still asleep in their bunks, and had slept through the whole traumatic episode. Rather sleepily — and possibly even annoyed at being disturbed from their slumbers — they too were removed from their comfortable bunks and forcibly assisted to escape from a watery grave.

In the event, they might as well have been left to sleep on in peace, for the vessel succeeded in riding out the storm. She went on to carve out a name for herself as the *Seedler* in the First World War, when, converted by the Germans into a commerce raider, she did a great deal of damage to Allied shipping. In the end she was wrecked yet again on an island in the South Seas, after being chased dramatically by naval vessels.

In another wreck on January 1st, 1916, the crew were even more reluctant to be saved and assisted to make their escape. When the steamship *Dunvegan* went ashore in Oxwich Bay near Pennard, the lifeboat — the same *Janet* we have met previously — was launched as the vessel was dragging her anchor and was likely to be blown onto the rocks.

'We put to sea in a big gale to go to a barque off Pwll du,' George Edmunds has recorded in the words of one of the survivors of this incident, Will Howell. '. . . Us made up fine, with wind following and sea a bit abeam. When us got to vessel she didn't want no help — pilot was what she wanted.

' "Damn you," says Billy crosslike (Billy was the Cox). "Us have left our teas for you, you and your pilot can go to Davy Jones for all of me," — shouting he was, along of the gale and the dark.'

Tragically, this comic situation was to end with the deaths of three of the lifeboat's crewmen. Will Howell continues his story:

'T'was when we put about she went over on us. John, he wanted to run afore the wind to Mumbles, but Billy he wanted to get home to he's bed where he said he did properly belong. First time she rolled over we lost two men. Old Grove come up alongside, "Leave me," said he, but Willy Grove, his son, pulled he inboard. We put her up into the wind but she got broadside — awkward cow she was in a seaway — and over she went again, t'was a finisher. When she came right side up along of them buoyancy tanks, most of us was in her but three was gone. Us was daunted proper when us did get home along.'

These simple words express far more of the courage and gallantry of all who try to rescue survivors from a wreck, particularly the lifeboatmen. On this particular occasion, after being called out in error by a ship which did not want their services, the crew of the lifeboat had to remain at sea for nearly 21 hours until they were able to make Mumbles and get ashore, having lost three of their comrades, with the remainder suffering from exposure. The Port Einon station was closed down afterwards, and this was a sad day for the *Janet*, which was removed from service and stored until she went to the Outer Hebrides in 1918.

As for the lifeboatmen who had been in the crew — as always, they were still there if ever and whenever they were needed.

Chapter Ten
Lifeboats to the Rescue

In the great days of sail when there were many flourishing ports in Wales which have now declined — the slate-exporting port of Porthmadog, and the smaller ones of Pwllheli and Barmouth, for instance — the natural hazards of the coast as well as human error brought many a tall ship to her grave. One of the worst was the notorious St Patrick's Causeway, which juts out from the land for some miles not far from Barmouth. Vessel after vessel came to grief on the causeway, and there were other equally dangerous hazards, traps for the unwary.

In the early days, the best sort of protection that could be offered to warn sailors of their dangers was in the form of a lighthouse — often just a beacon. In 1716, for instance, a coal-burning light was built by private enterprise on the Skerries, those treacherous rocks just north of Holyhead. Other lighthouses were built up and down the Welsh coast in the years that followed.

There was an ever-increasing need for safe harbours, havens for shipping, and for some means of gaining assistance if a ship did find herself in difficulties. But by the late 1840s, the only safe anchorage along the whole of the North Wales coast was the newly constructed harbour of refuge at Holyhead.

Beginnings in the direction of safety had already been made some 50 years before, however, when various ideas were put forward for 'life-saving apparatus', comprising of a mortar which fired a cannon ball or shot, attached to a chain or coil of rope. By firing the line across the stricken vessel, this made it possible to get a rope from the ship to the shore, and in 1815, the apparatus invented by a boyhood friend of Nelson, Captain George Manby — a sort of popgun — was ordered by the House of Commons to be provided at forty-five sites which had especially bad records so far as wrecks were concerned. Included in these sites were Point Lynas, Great Orme and Point of Ayr on the North Wales coast.

Later, rockets replaced the mortars, and some sixty-five years further on, there were 195 stations boasting the more up to date 'life saving apparatus', otherwise known as 'coast rescue equipment', along the coasts of England and Wales. These played a vital role, as we have seen, on many occasions when a ship was wrecked or in difficulties. The original "Manby's Mortar" saved the lives of more than one thousand people during the inventor's lifetime — a record to be proud of.

In the 1860s, the new Boxer Rocket was introduced to shoot a line out to a stricken ship, and it must have been regarded as a miracle of modern science. Each rocket had a double charge, the first to take off and the second, which ignited as the rocket sped forward, to add extra thrust and thus provide a much greater range than previous equipment had been able to do. This remained in service for almost a hundred years, to be superseded by the modern rescue rocket which is in use today. This was tested at the Pendine range in 1947 by an Inspector of H.M. Coastguards Western Division, Mr Ted Williams of Swansea.

Coastguards today have other means of rescue at their disposal, including cliff scaling equipment and air-sea rescue helicopters. But the best known method of rescuing survivors from a wreck, and the one which has occasioned stories which ring back over the years with accounts of heroism and drama and gallantry, is of course that of the lifeboats.

So far as Wales was concerned, as far back as 1783, the historian Henry Parry informs us, 'the Druidical Society of Anglesey offered £10 to any farmer on the coasts of Anglesey, Caernarfonshire or Merioneth who gave the greatest assistance with men and horses to save life from any vessel wrecked in the neighbourhood.'

We may imagine that this offer was received with scorn by those who had banded themselves into wrecking and smuggling gangs, but there were many honest people who were more concerned with saving life than with plunder. And in the 1820s, the rector of Llanfair-yng-Nghornwy, the Reverend James Williams (whom we have previously encountered in these pages riding on horseback to save five lives from the *Active* and being awarded the first RNLI Gold Medal ever to come to Wales) and his wife Frances Williams, began their efforts to found what was to become the Anglesey Association for the Preservation of Life from Shipwreck.

They were not the only people who were concerned with trying to save life from the sea. At about the same time, Sir William Hillary was busy at his home in Douglas, Isle of Man, preparing a pamphlet which was published in 1823 as: 'An appeal to the British Nation on the Humanity and Policy of Forming a National Institution for the Preservation of Lives and Property from Shipwreck.' Out of this was to grow the modern-day RNLI.

Frances Williams is one of Wales' great heroines, a lady of compassion, courage and enterprise. As a girl growing up near the Welsh coast, she heard accounts of the terrible disasters to shipping and wrecks on the cruel rocks on dark nights, if she did not actually view such scenes for herself. But on March 26, 1823, as a young married woman, she — and possibly her husband too — was a witness of the wreck of the Irish sailing packet *Alert* which went aground on the rocks known as the West Mouse between the Skerries and Cemlyn.

The *Alert* was not wrecked in the dark hours, with wind howling through the rigging and the seas running high. She became becalmed on a fine windless day, on her way from Howth to Parkgate, and in full view of those on the shore only a mile away, she drifted, in the pull of the strong tide that ran between the Skerries and the mainland, onto the rocks, unable to save herself.

The tragedy was all the greater because the ship, being a packet boat, was crowded with people. She sank almost immediately after going aground and holing herself and it was later discovered that 145 lives had been lost. Only seven people managed to reach safety in one of the ship's boats, and only another twenty-seven bodies were ever recovered.

The horror of the tragedy haunted Frances Williams. The reason why nothing had been able to be done to assist the packet and save those on board her, had been because there was no boat available to go to her aid, or the aid of any other stricken vessel. If only, Frances thought — as did many of the people with whom she discussed her ideas — some sort of life-saving boat could be provided, which would be on hand if a ship needed assistance. Such a boat could save the lives which were now, unavoidably, lost if a vessel ran into difficulties. And even if all those on board were not able to be saved, at least a tragedy like that of the *Alert* could be greatly lessened.

Enterprisingly, she began to raise money. In 1821, she had been present in Holyhead when King George IV landed there after his state visit to Ireland, and she had painted a picture of the scene. This she had lithographed and from the sale of the copies, she raised the substantial sum of nearly £60. She used the money to start a fund called the King's Landing Fund, which rewarded efforts made to help save life at sea, and encouraged future activities in this direction.

In the meantime, in March 1824, the Royal National Institution for the Preservation of Life from Shipwreck was founded. By 1850, about a hundred lifeboats were in existence — and most of them in service — around the coasts of Britain. Thirty of these belonged to the Institution, and the rest were provided by societies such as that which was founded by Frances Williams and her husband, the culmination of their efforts towards saving life from the sea.

On the foundation of the RNLI (as the Institution was to be re-named in 1854) Frances and her husband and their co-workers for safety at sea immediately pledged their support. Frances urged her husband to write making himself known and telling of their own efforts, which resulted in a regular and stimulating exchange of information and correspondence passing between the little Anglesey rectory and the offices of the Institution.

In 1828, largely as a result of Frances Williams' unceasing efforts in this direction, the first lifeboat on the North Wales coast was delivered to be stationed at Cemlyn, which became the first operational lifeboat station in North Wales. Frances and her husband enthusiastically raised more funds for another boat — locally-built — to be stationed at Holyhead, and in December of that year they organised a public meeting in Beaumaris where they were able to see the fruition at long last of their most dearly cherished hopes and dreams to help alleviate disaster at sea around their own coasts.

At the public meeting on December 10, 1828, the Anglesey Association for the Preservation of Life from Shipwreck was formed, with the Reverend James Williams as its first treasurer. Later of course, this and other similar local organisations were to become incorporated into the RNLI, but in the meantime, they did sterling work as separate bodies in helping to save life at sea. In the years before the Anglesey Life-saving Association (as it was also called) became a branch of the RNLI, the island's lifeboats and other means of life-saving, such as the Manby apparatus, were responsible for saving nearly 600 lives.

The trouble was that, though there was a great deal of goodwill, not only the lifeboats themselves but the ships they were pledged to save — particularly in the years before the RNLI took over all the existing lifeboat stations round the coasts of Britain, and pledged to keep the boats manned and in good repair — were often safety hazards. Owners would too many times neglect repairs or safety precautions in favour of making extra speed on a voyage, or carrying a cargo that over-loaded the vessel — or simply to save spending money.

One of the most notorious wrecks off the Welsh coast which became tragically disastrous due in a large part to lack of safety precautions and sea-worthiness of the vessel itself, was that of the *Rothsay Castle*, a paddle-steamer which plied a day-trip trade between Liverpool and Beaumaris. On August 18, 1831, in bad weather, she went aground on Dutchman's Bank in Beaumaris Bay, and broke her back.

The vessel had originally been built to serve along the Clyde, and when she arrived in Liverpool, she was already a tired, underpowered ship which should never have put to sea again. In fact, it is reported that several of the prospective crew refused point blank to sail in her — and one of them later had this refusal accepted by the Manchester Commissioners in Lunacy as undisputable proof that the man had been sane at the time.

Apart from material facts that the ship's only boat had no oars and a hole in the bottom, that there was no signal gun, and that the timbers were rotting, it was common knowledge among the sea-going fraternity that this vessel was far from seaworthy. In addition, rumour had it that the officers were quarrelsome and often drunk. But unfortunately, most of these grave drawbacks were not evident to the 150 day-trippers who crowded on board on that fateful morning of August 17, and felt the ship judder beneath them when she headed out to sea round about mid-day.

Once at sea, the *Rothsay Castle* took the full force of strong winds and heavy seas, and soon even the bandsmen who had been playing for the pleasure of the passengers, were crippled with sea-sickness. The passengers were, not surprisingly, becoming increasingly alarmed and a deputation went below to request the captain to return to Liverpool. They were met, however, with horrible oaths and instructions to keep out and stop interfering, from a captain who was well and truly drunk.

By 5 o'clock, when Captain Atkinson at last came on deck, the ship was letting in water. He had no more useful contribution to make to the wellbeing of the passengers, however, than to say darkly that 'This night will tell a tale', and allow the poor *Rothsay Castle* to plod on in the heavy seas. By ten o'clock in the evening, the ship passed the Great Orme — a mere thirty-six miles from their starting-place in Liverpool — but those aboard who were hoping to make Beaumaris very shortly had their hopes dashed when, within sight of Puffin Island, one of the firemen came on deck to report two feet of water in the stokehold.

Unless the ship was to run out of steam, somebody had to man the pumps — so the long-suffering passengers were ordered below. The pumps, however, like so many other things on the ship, did not work, so in desperation, the male passengers tried to form a chain and bail the water out with buckets. This bright idea was soon squashed when they were informed that the only bucket on the ship had fallen overboard.

What might have seemed farcical in the extreme, however, soon turned to real tragedy when the ship was caught on the Dutchman's Bank. The captain once again displayed his shiftlessness in a position of command and his propensity for blaming others whenever things went wrong; he cursed the helmsman, claiming that the latter had never known how to steer, and then, notwithstanding that the fires were out below so that there was no steam, he ordered the ship 'full astern'. Since she was not able to answer to any orders at all, she continued to bump on across the treacherous sands that formed the Dutchman's Bank for another mile or so. Then she began to break up.

The funnel was first to go, taking the main-mast along with it. The side of the ship was smashed in, and the captain was among those swept to their death. Many of the passengers had been lashed to the mast for safety, and were unable to escape — it was a terrible end to what had begun as a pleasure trip with the band playing and the bunting flying.

There were only twenty-three survivors of the wreck. Nine of them, including one lone woman, drifted on what remained of the poop, using the lady's skirts as a sail. Others clung to pieces of wreckage. When morning came and the terrible plight of the *Rothsay Castle* could be seen from the shore, boats put out to pick up the survivors, but there was on this occasion no lifeboat that might have come to the assistance of the doomed ship.

As a result of the tragedy, however, the Anglesey Lifesaving Association set up a lifeboat station at Penmon in the following year, and in response to an application to the Government, a new lighthouse was built at Penmon, completed in 1838.

Often, the brave crew of a lifeboat has given its own lives in attempting to carry out its rescue work. The Mumbles lifeboat is one such. Established in 1835, it achieved national — if not international — fame on the occasion of the wreck of the *Prinz Adalbert* in 1883, which as we have heard, was immortalised in the dramatic poem 'The Women of Mumbles Head'.

On February 1, 1903, the current Mumbles lifeboat was a self-righting type of boat, 35 feet long, which had cost £765 to build. She had been provided, as were many of the lifeboats, as part of a legacy, this time from Mr J. Stevens of Birmingham, and it comes as no surprise to hear that she was named *James Stevens No 12*.

The lifeboat was launched on February 1, 1903, to go to the assistance of the *Christine* of Waterford, which had grounded off Port Talbot. Her help was not required, however, so the crew of the *James Stevens No 12* made for the harbour at Port Talbot. It was a calm day, but people who were watching saw in horror that just outside the harbour entrance, a freak wave caught the lifeboat and overturned her.

She righted herself, but the same thing happened again almost immediately, and six of the crew of fourteen were washed overboard. The ship was dashed against the rocks and damaged beyond repair, but by what seemed a miracle, the remaining crew members survived, — never to forget, however, their comrades, all six of whom met their death either from drowning or being battered to death.

On April 23, 1947, the 7000 ton steamer *Samtampa* en route from Middlesborough to Newport, was at anchor in Swansea Bay, having been driven there in a gale which, by evening, had turned to a 70-mile-per-hour hurricane. Her anchor cables snapped and she soon found herself wrecked on Sker Point, off Porthcawl.

The Mumbles lifeboat set out to go to her assistance, but, unable to locate her, returned to Mumbles for more precise details as to the whereabouts of the stricken ship, and made a second attempt at about eight in the evening. Gallantly, she disappeared into the dark of night and tempest — and that was the last that anyone saw of her until the awful scene which was revealed when the day dawned the next morning.

The *Samtampa* had been driven hard against the rocks, and had quickly broken up. No-one had been able to reach her, and the rockets which the rocket crew had tried to fire had been driven back by the high winds. By morning, she lay in several pieces, every one of her crew of 39 gone. The gallant little lifeboat was intact, but floating nearby upside down. Each member of her crew of 8 was missing — all lost. In their efforts to assist a ship in distress, they had sacrificed their own lives.

Many other lifeboatman has willingly given his all in the constant fight to save life from the sea, and international regulations have made safety precautions a part of regular sea-going routine. And when the dark nights and heavy seas throw a vessel onto the rocks, or if the person in distress is a small boy, clinging terrified to a dinghy as it is swept out to sea, those who man the lifeboats know that their sacrifice is not in vain — that each time their boat is launched, they will have helped to swell the numbers of those who would otherwise have been lost perhaps without trace, victims of the deep. By the Grace of God and the courage of the lifeboatmen, many who would otherwise have died are saved every year from the sea.

Chapter Eleven
Cursed!

It may be fanciful to say that some ships seem to be cursed, to sail under a sort of cloud of doom, yet there have been cases which appear to suggest that the sad end of the vessel was inevitable, that it was the curse which rested upon it that drove it to its awful fate.

Take the story of the mystery ship that is said to have been stranded in the Burry Estuary in the dim past. According to local tradition, the survivors somehow made their way ashore, and climbed the cliffs in the dark hours of night. They stumbled upon the village of Llanelen, and were warmly welcomed by the villagers. Food and shelter were provided, and the villagers generously gave of their own meagre fare, to help these wrecked seamen.

Little did they know — possibly the sailors themselves did not know — that the stranded vessel was a plague ship. It is reported that within only a few days, most of the villagers had succumbed to the deadly menace which the sailors had carried with them. The village of Llanelen became a 'ghost village' and fell into ruins, of which there is now little remaining except for a few stones. The only evidence that it existed is in the form of two very old stones from Llanelen Church, one dating from 1687, which were built into the churchyard gatepost at Llanrhidian.

The only ghost which is said to walk as a result of the tragedy is a lady in white, who, according to tradition, haunts the place where the lost village once stood. We can imagine, however, that on a dark night, it would be only too easy to think that the dim shape of the plague ship that had brought such devastation with it to the Welsh coast, might be visible just off-shore in the estuary, too fearful a sight to be approached.

Another vessel that seemed to be mysteriously cursed was the *Ann of Bridgwater*, which was seen drifting in Rhosili Bay on December 31st, 1899, heading for the shore. The Rhosili rocket crew, who had been alerted by signals of distress, tried to get a line to the stricken ship, but there seemed to be no crew aboard to make the line fast. They waited until the tide ebbed, and then the coastguard and District Officer Captain Allen boarded the apparently empty vessel.

To their astonishment, they found no living being on board except for the ship's cat. And what seemed even more mysterious was that the papers of the ship's captain gave the captain's name, age and height as exactly those of Captain Allen himself!

In fact, the mystery was not as interesting as might appear, for it emerged that the crew had already been taken off when the vessel got into difficulties, and had been safely transported to Llanelli. But there were more dramatic incidents on this seeming ghost ship before she was finally abandoned.

The coastguard and Captain Allen and their men decided that they would salvage the ship themselves, so they remained on board and waited for the tide to turn. They made themselves at home, making a stew which was declared 'grand' by coastguard Reeves, who had liberally flavoured his plateful with pepper from the pepper box. When Captain Allen inspected the pepper box before peppering his own plateful, however, he discovered that far from containing pepper, it was in fact full of Keatings Insect Powder, which was 'warranted to kill bugs, lice and beetles'!

Poor coastguard Reeves, on realising he had eaten a plateful of this deadly powder, imagined that his last moment had come, and that he was about to expire on the spot. He did survive, however, but several hours later, when the tug that had been sent for had still not arrived, the rescue party had to abandon ship as the tide was now in and breaking in heavy waves over the vessel. It is safe to say that, with one thing and another, they were glad to leave the strangely cursed *Ann Of Bridgwater* for the haven of secure dry land. Within twenty-four hours, she had broken up completely and the wreckage was scattered along the shore.

On the last day of August, 1908, a gale swept the Irish Sea, and an alert from lighthouse keepers along the northern Anglesey coast caused the Cemlyn lifeboat crew to launch their boat in the teeth of the howling tempest. A ship had been glimpsed drifting eastward, but she had since disappeared into the darkness, and though both the Cemlyn lifeboat and the lifeboat from Bull Bay searched all through the long black night, tossed by the tempest and the high seas so that they were risking their lives at every moment, it was not until morning that they finally ran the mysterious vessel to ground. She had come to rest in the narrow channel inside the West Mouse rocks.

But when the lifeboatmen boarded her, they found her to be yet another apparent 'ghost ship'. Completely empty of all signs of human life, she had drifted with no hand save — they might well have imagined — some phantom hand at the helm all through that night while the lifeboats had been trying to locate her.

But the truth was, of course, much more prosaic. The lost vessel was the schooner *Flower of Portsoy*, which had been en route from Kinsale to Garston with a cargo of timber when the gale struck her. She had almost come to grief on the Skerries, by which time both anchors and her sails were gone, when the order came to abandon ship. The crew of four had lowered a boat, managed to get into it safely, and set to rowing grimly for the shore.

This was no easy task with the howling wind and high seas threatening to swamp them, and eventually they were literally thrown onto the beach by gigantic waves, which cast the boat ashore as though it was a piece of matchwood. The survivors managed to locate a nearby farm, where they were given food and warm dry clothing and shelter for the night. But in the meantime, the ship they had abandoned refloated herself — largely due to her cargo of timber — and began to drift on her aimless voyage which was to end when she was boarded by the lifeboatmen the next morning.

In the event, the new 'crew' found some extra sails which they managed to rig. They escorted the vessel, tugged by the *Olive* which arrived on the scene later in the day, back to Holyhead, and for their part in the salvage of the ship, both the lifeboat crews received a substantial amount of salvage money, which was very well deserved.

Yet another vessel which seemed to be cursed with the mysterious emptiness of a 'ghost ship' was the fishing boat *Pansy*, which drifted ashore at Kitchen Corner during the night of May 1st, 1941. When the dawn came, the coastguard discovered the vessel in five feet of water, partly submerged. The birds wheeled and screamed in the still early dawn light, and we can imagine that the coastguard, however down to earth a man he might have been, would have felt the hair on his neck crawl as he investigated the derelict vessel and found it quite deserted.

Even the fishing nets were thrown over the side as though the fishermen had been in the action of going about their work when the same mysterious something which haunts the ghost ships of this world, spirited them away.

In fact, of course, the answer was not that some supernatural force was at work, but that the crew of two had already been rescued. By the time the coastguard who discovered the boat was aware that they were safe, however, the *Pansy* had been completely wrecked.

Next to slaves, one of the most notorious human cargoes which was carried by any vessel was of 'pressed men' — men who had been snatched by the Press Gangs to serve under duress in Admiralty vessels. Often they were taken while going about their normal business, and they were not given time to inform their families what had happened to them. Shoved down in the recesses of the hold, crammed together and sometimes handcuffed, they were swiftly transported away from their homes and all that they held dear within hours of the Press Gangs having reaped their awful toll of living men.

Little wonder that a ship carrying a cargo of 'pressed men' might have been regarded as cursed, and that if she did come to grief, the populace in general might consider she had met her rightful fate.

Fear of the Press Gang ran high. It is recorded that 125 recruits for the Navy were raised by the twelve officers and men who were on impress service in Swansea in 1779, and the historian George Edmunds tells us that: 'When men were desperately needed, it was not uncommon for them to seek out their victims far beyond the town limits and it is on record that local men along the coast would hide in the caves during the periods of hot press.'

There is one account of a meeting between the Press Gang and some of the local men on the sands near Blackpill. John Voss of Nicholaston, and his neighbour John Smith, were returning from Swansea when they were accosted by a Press Gang consisting of twelve sailors and a Lieutenant. When they attempted to resist being 'pressed', fierce fighting took place and Voss's arm was almost severed at the shoulder, but he had managed to knock the Lieutenant down before he fell. The advent of his brother and two other men helped to put paid to the rest of the gang, and Voss was taken to Swansea, where his ghastly wounded arm received attention. Afterwards, he was allowed to go home.

The Press Gang had come from the Admiralty tender *Caesar*, en route from Bristol to Plymouth in that November of 1760. Together with another tender, the *Reeves*, she sailed from Mumbles Roads down the Channel on the morning of November 28, 1760, carrying at least 68 'pressed men' in the dark squalor of her hold. The state of the tide and the worsening state of the weather caused both ships to try and turn back to Mumbles, however.

A headland on the port bow, just visible in the distance in the poor light, loomed as a landmark. They mistakenly took it to be Mumbles Head, whereas in fact it was Pwll Du Head. And when the depths were sounded, the pilot made another error, thinking they were entering the shallows around Mumbles Head.

All too soon, the *Caesar* crashed terrifyingly, tearing her sides out on the rocks, while heavy seas broke over her. She stuck fast, and what survivors there were only managed to reach safety by climbing precariously along the bowsprit to the rocks, and thence up the cliffs. By morning, when the news that there had been a wreck had spread, crowds of local people flocked to the scene, to see mingled bodies and wreckage strewn in the blood-stained breakers.

Because the 'pressed men' were shut in the hold, many handcuffed, they could not escape and were drowned by the rising tide. All along the shore, the ghastly harvest of bodies gleaned from the sea was scattered — and as fate would have it, John Voss, who had rushed to the shore with the other local people, recognised the officer who had nearly severed his arm at their fateful encounter on Swansea sands, his sword now stilled for ever.

According to the captain of the *Caesar*, Adam Drake, at least sixty-eight people lost their lives in the wreck, and among the items salvaged from the wreckage were large numbers of guns — 44 muskets, 31 damaged musket barrels, 10 stock pieces, 27 pistols, 50 swords, 23 scabbards and 7 pole axes. More guns were retrieved in the months that followed.

All told, this was a sinister vessel, transporting as it did large numbers of 'pressed men' under duress, and heavily armed. Its end on the rocks near Pwll Du Head might well be considered in keeping with its violent nature.

A vessel which was cursed in the worst sense was the *Catherine Jenkins*, a barque whose home port was Swansea. She regularly sailed to Cuba for copper ore, as did many other Swansea barques, and one of the things their crews learned to dread was 'Yellow Jack', as they nicknamed the terrible yellow fever which killed off many of them. They even referred to Santiago as 'Swansea Cemetery', since so many Welshmen on this run perished there.

In the Autumn of 1856, the *Catherine Jenkins* sailed on her regular run with sixteen men on board. While she was at anchor in Cuba, the 'Yellow Jack' attacked the crew so that five of them died, leaving a crew of eleven to tackle the voyage home when she sailed on Christmas Eve. It was a foggy February night when she attempted to anchor in Mumbles Roads, and she struck the headland at a point between Lucas Bay and Oxwich Point.

The unfortunate crew tried to escape in the ship's boat, but no sooner had they all scrambled on board than they were thrown into the sea as the boat capsized. Four survivors managed to reach the shore safely — the rest, including the Captain, perished in the waves. The ship herself broke up, and the ore that she carried was brought to the foot of the cliff to be transported from there to the copper works. 'Even today,' says George Edmunds, 'vegetation is loathe to grow on the spot where the ore lay.'

There might well be a more prosaic reason for this lack of vegetation, but the lively mind will immediately assume that it was the terrible 'Yellow Jack' that this plague vessel had brought with her from Cuba, which, as in the case of the lost village, marked this corner of the coast as cursed for ever.

Chapter Twelve
In Song and Story

The wrecks of Wales have often been the inspiration for stirring and tragic laments or other works of literature, apart from many 'artists impressions' and stark photographs interpreting the drama of such scenes.

Not all the verses and songs composed as a result of these inspirations reach a wide audience. Yet, as in the case of the brigantine *Favorite* of Aberdyfi, the modest verse written as a result of the tragic occurrences in connection with this vessel by an unassuming man — the licensee of an inn — still lives today.

It happened on February 27, 1839. The ship was at anchor, prepared to sail the following day from Aberdyfi, and the crew had invited four girls, Ann Felix, the 17-year-old daughter of the licensee of the Britannia Inn, and three others who were all members of Mrs Scott's Boarding School for Young Ladies at Penhelig — on board for a special goodbye supper. The captain of the vessel had discreetly turned a 'blind eye' to such frolics aboard his vessel, and removed himself from the scene. After all, once they sailed, his crew would not see any ladies for a very long time.

On the evening in question, three of the crew, Owen Williams, John Angel and an apprentice identified only as Lewis from Tywyn, rowed ashore in the ship's boat and found the girls ready and waiting at the Britannia Inn as had been arranged. The fourth crew member, carpenter Edward Thomas, was to join them, but by 7 o'clock, he had not arrived — in fact, he was having trouble with his horse — so the others decided to wait no longer, but to leave for their own festivities.

It was the proprietress of the Boarding School for Young Ladies, Mrs Scott, who made the awful discovery, hours later, that three of her girls were missing, and made frantic efforts to trace them. She questioned their companions, and hurried off to the Britannia Inn. Ann Felix had not returned either, and a boat was sent at once to the *Favorite*.

In the best traditions of tragic drama, the brigantine was utterly deserted, with the table still waiting, laid for that sumptuous goodbye feast which the crew and their ladies were to have enjoyed. Now, the feast would remain for ever un-eaten, for by the time the next day dawned, the ship's boat, in which the laughing party had departed from the quayside the previous evening, was discovered wrecked at the mouth of the estuary. And scattered over a distance of several miles, the bodies of the three crewmen and their guests were washed up on the beaches. It is even recorded that the body of one of the Young Ladies was swept up the estuary for two miles, and came to rest at last near her home at Tafolgraig.

The unfortunate Ann Felix was buried in Tywyn churchyard, and on her tombstone was carved a verse which her father, Mine Host of the Britannia Inn, had written. In its simplicity, it captures all the heartbreak of this sad affair, one which was to prey so much on the mind of Mrs Scott that she died the following year.

Ann's father wrote:

'Weep not for me, my parents dear,
I am not dead, but sleeping here;
Prepare, prepare to follow me
You cannot prepare too soon;
For the night did come
Before I thought it noon.'

One wreck whose fame was to resound far beyond the coasts of Wales was that of the *Cyprian* in 1881. This tale of heroism, tragedy and — it was even claimed later — cowardice and failure to perform their duty by the Porthdinllaen lifeboat crew — became the subject of a sermon preached in Westminster Abbey when the heroic facts became known.

The hero of this wreck was the commander of the vessel, Captain John Alexander Strachan, who was at the helm when his ship left Liverpool for Genoa on the afternoon of October 13, 1881. Late that night, having run into a gale, she was somewhere in Caernarfon Bay when she had an almost unbelievable series of misfortunes. First, one of her engines burst, but by using the other, the Captain managed to keep the vessel bows-on to the gale until the next morning.

At half past eight, however, the steam steering-gear failed. Further, we are told by Ivor Wynne Jones: 'a cogwheel then snapped in the hand-steering system, leaving the captain with no alternative but to lash the helm and rely entirely upon his one engine, until water entered the furnace depriving the *Cyprian* of all power.'

The only things that might save the ship from disaster now, were her two anchors. At three in the afternoon, when they sighted land, the Captain took soundings, and dropped the port anchor. But due to some bungling sailor's failure to apply the brake on the windlass at the right moment, the port anchor ran away with all its chain. And when the starboard anchor was dropped, the chain snapped. This meant that nothing could stop the ship now from wrecking herself on the shore, and the crew began to prepare itself for what lay ahead.

Lifejackets were hastily donned — but there was one youngster aboard who had no lifejacket. His name was J.W. Khalan, and he had in fact been stowing away on the *Cyprian* but, realising the ship was not a safe place any longer, he had made his presence known.

When the Captain saw him, he immediately took off his own lifejacket and gave it to the lad. He is recorded as saying: 'Here you are, take mine, I'll swim for it.' And at half past five in the afternoon, when the vessel struck some two miles from Porthdinllaen, she began to break up at once, so her crew found themselves all struggling to survive as they were swept away in the breakers.

As luck would have it, the Captain never reached the shore alive. He and eighteen members of his crew were drowned, but the stowaway to whom he had given his life-jacket was one of eight who did survive.

The heroism of Captain Strachan inspired more than the sermon which was later preached in Westminster Abbey; funds for a lifeboat to serve on the coast where the wreck had occurred were donated to the RNLI by a Mrs Noble of Henley-on-Thames, and the boat, named

Cyprian, served at the new lifeboat station of Trefor. An inquiry was held at Nefyn in order to silence the storm of outrage that was directed at the Porthdinllaen lifeboat, which had made no attempt to rescue the vessel or her crew, and it was publicly established that those on the shore had good reason from the erratic behaviour of the vessel, to think she had been abandoned, also that even if the lifeboat had tried to effect a rescue, there was nothing that could have been done to avert the tragedy.

The gallant Captain Strachan was taken to be buried in Liverpool, while the other victims of the wreck lie in Edern churchyard.

As for the local people, many of them had risked their lives on the rocks in trying to give a helping hand to the survivors in the sea. They were rewarded for their bravery: Nanhoron squire gave each a gold sovereign, a medal and a certificate at a celebration held in their honour.

Years later, there was to be a dramatic postscript to the story of the *Cyprian*. Captain William Roberts of Llanengan was saved from the sea when his ship sank near the Azores. He was taken on board the *Highland Watch*, and was amazed to find that the Chief Steward of the vessel which had rescued him was none other than the stowaway to whom Captain Strachan had given his own lifejacket on the night when the Cyprian sank!

Rather surprisingly, various wrecks off the Welsh coast have been set as the subject for poems or other literary compositions at eisteddfodau — Welsh competitions for artistic skill and talent. Obviously, it was felt that the subjects of the wrecks would cause the competitiors to rise on wings of inspiration.

That of the disastrous paddle-steamer *Rothsay Castle*, which broke up on the Dutchman's Bank after attempting to take 150 passengers on a day trip to Beaumaris, as we have heard in a previous chapter, was set as the subject for a most important competiton — an ode. The occasion was the North Wales Eisteddfod, which was held at Beaumaris Castle in the year following the tragedy, 1832, and which was attended by the Princess Victoria and her mother, the Duchess of Kent.

The ode was the main competition of the eisteddfod, and nineteen competitors felt that they had something to say on the subject of the wreck of the *Rothsay Castle*. And just so that the Princess Victoria would not forget about it either, she received a presentation set of drawings of 'artists impressions' of the tragedy, all tastefully bound in gold-trimmed morocco.

Much interest and strong emotion was aroused by the great losses of life in the various emigrant ships which never reached their destinations, not only in Wales, but in the Welsh colonies abroad. For instance, the subject for entries at the Aberaeron Eisteddfod in 1873 was the 'Sinking of the *Northfleet*'. This vessel had been hit by an unidentified steamer which did not stop or report the collision, and had gone down with 293 emigrants. It was as a result of this tragedy that it became a legal necessity for all British ships to carry their names on the stern and both sides of the bows, clearly marked. The people around Cardigan Bay would surely have supported the eisteddfod with this tragedy as its principal theme, and honoured the poet who produced the best composition.

In 1874, a year after the Aberaeron Eisteddfod, a similar theme was set for entries for the Utica Eisteddfod in the USA. This time the theme was the 'Wrecking of the *Atlantic*' and commemorated the loss of 546 emigrants when the White Star's *Atlantic* went aground near Halifax, Nova Scotia, en route to New York in April, 1873.

But possibly the most celebrated method of setting up a memorial to a particular wreck was the one which was done by the sailors themselves — the composing of a sea shanty. In the early years of this century, Professor J. Glyn Davies, of the University of Liverpool, published his life-long work in the field of identifying and saving authentic old songs which had been sung by Welsh sailors, and we can almost hear those haunting voices as the men went about their duties — singing the different types of shanties which were dictated by what they were doing — a 'halliard' as opposed to a 'capstan' shanty, for instance.

Often there might be half a dozen or more versions of a good shanty, and one which achieved immortality in this respect was the story of Captain Huw Puw, whose 60-ton flat, the *Ann* (or the *Ann Puw*) was wrecked on St Tudwal's Islands on October 18, 1858. The little ship was en route to Barmouth with a cargo of timber when the tragedy happened, and there was nothing spectacular about either the disaster or any rescues which might have been effected, to make it an occasion to remember. Yet the different versions of shanties about the *Fflat Huw Puw* have resounded round the world, wherever Welshman sailed.

One version, of which only one stanza still survives, portrays the little ship fighting her way through the waters where she was to come to grief, with says Ivor Wynne Jones: '63-year-old Capt. Pugh struggling at the tiller and crying loud for divine assistance.'

Professor J. Glyn Davies' collections of shanties bring back the old days of sail with colourful richness. We can picture those Welsh sailors, swaggering their way round the ports they visited, and yet, when singing in three-part harmony, with unbearable beauty in their voices. Many of the shanties came from the west, from America, and as Professor Glyn Davies tells us: 'I myself recollect how many Welsh shellbacks had picked up American tunes whilst loading cotton in the Southern States in the old days. There was even a cultivation of a Yankee accent by Welsh seamen, and I cannot call to mind many of my old seafaring friends entirely free from it.'

In the old days, songs and ballads telling of wrecks were often sung at market crosses by travelling singers who spread the news, whether it was good or bad, in the same way as a newspaper does now. It was only by word of mouth that the dreadful happenings on the coast came to be known inland, and ship-wrecks, like murder stories, were fascinatingly told with the spellbound audience guaranteed to rush to buy the penny ballad-sheets at the end of the performance.

Chapter Thirteen

A Pilot on Board

As time went by, there grew up a class of pilots, who would board a vessel in order to navigate it through a dangerous water-way or approach to a harbour. Without a pilot on board, masters of ships were reluctant to try and tackle these difficult areas themselves.

Aled Eames tells us, for instance, that: 'The *Coast and Sailing Directions* for Anglesey compiled by Lieutenant Charles G. Robinson, R.N., and published in 1837 by Captain John Corden, R.N., drew the attention of mariners to the problems of navigation in the Menai Straits, particularly the Swellies, "no vessel is justified in attempting it without a pilot: who are a distinct class from either those at Penmon or Caernarfon: consequently a vessel going through the Strait is subject to three distinct Pilots".'

These men were a breed apart, but they were no less subject to the hazards which claimed unsuspecting ships whose masters did not know the waters so well. Their task was a dangerous and important one, and they were responsible for the safe passing of many souls and vessels which were placed in their care, sometimes at the risk of their own lives.

It is recorded, for instance, that 'On the 25 November 1826 the *Marquis of Wellington*, Liverpool to Bahia, parted her chain-cable at the entrance to Holyhead harbour, "during a tremendous gale from N.W., and drove upon the rocks at S.E. part of the Bay, where in a few minutes she went to pieces, and all on board, including a pilot belonging to this place, drowned".'

A document which has survived for over a century and is now kept at Anglesey County Library, is the log-book of one of the Anglesey pilots — Henry Edwards, Swellies Pilot, No. 8. He began his book with a flourish in January 1867, when he wrote (presumably, as Aled Eames has noted in his accounts of this interesting volume, for the sake of posterity):

> 'When I am dead and in my grave
> and all my bones are rotten
> Here's the book you'll see my name
> When I am quite forgotten.'

He kept his log-book faithfully for eleven years, noting down, as required, the names of the vessels he piloted through the Menai Straits and the fees he received, as well as other random information such as the state of the weather and anything that he found of note, including bits of verse, loans he made to friends, details of his wedding and often, births, deaths or accidents.

While these did sometimes include accounts of wrecks, they also mentioned less dramatic loss of life; for instance, he wrote on April 11, 1868: 'Calm, fine and clear, Colonel Williams, Graig y don, Vallat (valet) drowned by Bathing on a Sunday.' Mr Edwards was, we can gather from this, not a frivolous man, and one who was extremely pious about observing his Sundays.

His accounts of the wrecks are laconic — pilots were people who dealt with danger, and it was a part of their day-to-day living. Aled Eames has given us a few of his entries concerning various wrecks, such as:

> '20 July 1873, "American ship towed on beam ends to Penmon"; 25 March 1872, "Man lost from the Schooner *Madryn* off Portdinorwig"; 20 February 1869, "Northerly gale which Gale 21 vessels went ashore at Red Wharf, Anglesey, and the *Catherine* of Pwllheli swamp with all hands.'

Often the tragedies he recorded came closer to home. Of one of his fellow pilots, he wrote on 24 July 1869: "Jack Pierce's boat with his two lads when boarding the *Walter Dean* under the Britannia bridge capsized, Jack being near drowned." And on 24 June 1873: "The Garth boat capsized on Beaumaris Bank, Dick Hussar's daughter drowned." On 6 August 1873: "Jack Crow and Johnny White Lion Beaumaris drowned, the yacht *Dare* lost on Taylor's Bank Liverpool, one saved."

Often, various pilots found their work frustrating in the extreme. The Llanddwyn pilots living in houses which belonged to the Caernarfon Harbour Trust were paid five pounds extra each year for manning the lifeboat if this should be necessary, and in one bad November storm, they took the lifeboat out to try and find a schooner whose sails had been carried away, which they had glimpsed late in the afternoon, obviously in distress. When they returned, they penned this disgusted report:

> 'we poole back and fored till after 3 oclock in the morning, cant find the ship on count the ship wont anser our lights.'

But there were compensations to being a pilot. Henry Edwards recorded one of the high spots of his career at the back of his log-book, when he wrote that on September 5, 1879, he piloted the Queen's yacht *Vice Versa* safely. Other vessels of note which were placed in his hands, temporarily, were *HMS Royal Charlotte* and *HMS Tay*. And he has achieved the ambition he had in mind when he opened his log-book with a flourish and claimed his name would be remembered long after his bones were rotten. We can see him clearly in the mind's eye, working the Straits in those great days of Welsh shipping, piloting the schooner *Heir Apparent* and the *Menai Packet* and the *Amlwch Packet*, white sails through those waters he knew so well. It is safe to say that without the generations of pilots who have steered vessels through the rocks, reefs, currents and channels and all the other hazards round Wales' coasts, there would have been a far greater number of wrecks than did actually occur.

Chapter Fourteen
The Comic Side

One might imagine that there is very little that could possibly be funny about a wreck. But we have seen that often, side by side with the drama and the tragedy, run events or incidents which, in spite of the seriousness of the situation, make the onlooker smile in spite of himself.

What happened to the armed steamship *Eldon Park* in 1940 is a good example. She was on her way from North Africa to Port Talbot, carrying iron ore, when she hit a mine off Lundy, and before the master could carry out his intention of beaching her in Port Einon Bay, she sank during the night of February 7 in the middle of the bay. A dramatic rescue was effected by the Mumbles lifeboat when 37 men were saved from their precarious perch on the bridge, the only part of the vessel which remained above water. Seven times, the lifeboat ran in in very heavy seas, with floating wreckage a terrible danger, to take the men off, and the Coxwain, William Davies — who was later awarded the RNLI Thanks inscribed on Vellum — said afterwards that he had never known such cheering from rescued men as that which the crew of the *Eldon Park* set up once they had been safely transported to the shore. They gave the tired lifeboatmen a most marvellous and appreciative reception in thanks for the rescue.

But it was what happened afterwards which brought a touch of the light fantastic to this doomed ship. It was decided by the Ministry of

Information to use the wreck as the setting for a war-time film, and the actors and 'extras' collected as the cameras began to roll. Representing seamen on a 'torpedoed' vessel were the sea cadets from Swansea, as well as local men, all of whom were paid the princely sum of one pound per day, plus meals.

In order to make for interest and colour, some of the real seamen who were with the film unit unearthed a collection of funny beach hats that had not been sold during the previous summer season, and bought up the whole lot. They had already attired themselves in a strange collection of rough and ready clothes, and carried Verey light pistols at their belts, with which to fire smoke bombs on the wreck for an authentic atmosphere, and with the addition of the funny hats, they made a sight to strike panic into the stoutest heart.

Even though some of the hats did look familiar, the villagers who observed these incredible activities, and who had not been informed about the film, made haste to summon reinforcements — after all, there was a war on, and who knew what enemy spies or agents might not get up to? Piracy and looting seemed only the mildest and most harmless of the possible threats that might be facing the district.

Hot footing it to the scene of the crime, the Swansea CID arrived at top speed, and there must have been some red faces all round when the truth was revealed. It is to be hoped that the film itself was as entertaining as the events when it was being shot!

Often, it is the mysterious which can provide the most in the way of amusement. Among the records of the Barmouth lifeboat, for instance, there are some small details which, praiseworthy though they may be when considered apart, add up to a picture that suggests extremely amusing possibilities once they are put together.

The events happened in the years 1965 and 1966. The Barmouth lifeboat, *The Chieftain*, was called out on June 20, 1965, to the motor boat *Violet Sinclair* of Barmouth. Dramatic dashes to stranded crew were not on this occasion required, but it is on the record that the lifeboat 'gave help'. Back home went the *Violet Sinclair*, a sadder and, presumably, wiser vessel after her narrow escape. After all, lifeboats are not called out for nothing, and we can take it that *Violet* had certainly got herself into some sort of trouble.

But lo and behold, a mere three weeks later, on August 13, 1965, the lifeboat was called out once again — to the *Violet Sinclair*! This time it was necessary to save no less than four poeple who were in distress on board, though the boat seemingly managed to muddle through and survive intact from whatever the problem had been.

How do we know this? Because, in the following March the peril of the Barmouth seas was out again, and in trouble once more. On March 22, the records show that the lifeboat had to save not only the *Violet Sinclair* herself, but three people who were on board.

And, as a finale, on July 8, the long-suffering lifeboat crew went out yet again to save the *Violet Sinclair* and the four people aboard (who might well have been the same people as had been rescued previously).

Four calls out to the same vessel within two years is almost certainly a record among the annals of lifeboat history, and we cannot help but wonder what was the cause of this incredible course of events? Were the crew of the *Violet Sinclair* in a constant state of intoxication, so that whenever they went for a trip on the briny, they were incapable of handling the boat and were a danger to themselves and every other craft in sight? Was the skipper craftily trying to collect on his insurance money? Or had he made a cunning plan to dispose of his wife, but kept getting frustrated by the appearance of the lifeboat, which kept coming doggedly to the rescue? We shall probably never know, but the possibilities are endless — and endlessly and hilariously fascinating.

It is not surprising, human nature being what it is, that many of the comedies which were played out as a result of wrecks, concerned cargoes of brandy, wine or other intoxicating liquor. The people on the receiving end of a wreck were apparently able to resist the lure of coal, linens or various eatables that might have been stored in the hold — if it seemed advisable to do so — but they could never let pass a good wine or brandy, and got up to all sorts of escapades in order to make sure they did not miss out on the alcohol.

In the late Eighteenth Century, the *Providence* of Hastings was en route to London from Dublin when she went aground at Rhoscolyn carrying a cargo of wine, linen cloth, skin and a commodity oddly referred to as 'feathers'. Her crew were rescued by a team led by one Thomas Roberts of Bodior, who carried their boat on their shoulders for a quarter of a mile in order to get to the nearest launching point to the doomed vessel, and after Mr Roberts and his friends had satisfied themselves that none of the seamen were suffering from 'ye contagion in France', which they were anxious not to catch, they were put safely ashore.

The next day, Mr Lloyd, the Customs collector from Holyhead, arrived on the scene, and bossily instructed Mr Roberts to transport the wine which the ship had been carrying, away in his carts, otherwise 'all ye wine would be carryed off and drunk by the countrey people before the next morning.' Mr Roberts, smarting from having his prizes taken from him when it was he, after all, who had organised the rescue, must have protested against the Customs collector's high-handedness. Mr Lloyd began to huff and puff officiously, and declared he could cross 'any man's ground in ye King's name' in order to appropriate goods from a wreck.

Temper flaring, Mr Roberts seized a stick at this, and proceeded to call the Customs collector a few choice names, 'rascall, vilain' and 'scoundrel' being only some of the mildest. What might have developed is anyone's guess, but presumably the angry squabblers were calmed down by their more level-headed companions. Even though Mr Roberts and his friends went home, though, the matter was not allowed to drop, and claims and counter-claims were made for the wrecked wine before the justices of Llannerch-y-medd, by all concerned.

And Wales too has its own version of 'Whisky Galore'. In 1901, the *Stuart* went into difficulties near Porth Ty Mawr on the Llyn Peninsula. She was carrying a cargo of whisky, and lost most of it when she was wrecked. Naturally, all the locals rushed to the scene, and a great many of the bottles were emptied there and then, causing the spot to be christened 'Porth Wisgi'. So long as the whisky lasted, the locals continued to enjoy themselves, in spite of the frowns of the chapel authorities, and because they smashed the necks of the bottles in order to get at the precious liquor, there were some cut lips about as well as hangovers during the next few days.

Ballads were composed to celebrate the occasion, and local folklore even has it that some of the bottles — unopened — remain as souvenirs on the dressers in local houses even now.

In many cases, the wine was not so much wrecked, but smuggled. We have heard how the people of the coast often turned a blind eye to the smuggling that went on, or even participated in it, and where brandy or wine was concerned, they would go to great lengths to get it. Running battles were fought for years between the smugglers and the Customs officers, with the smugglers usually, according to tradition, coming off best.

It is said that William Arthur, leader of the most successful **gang of** smugglers ever to operate in Gower, once had a visit from some Customs officers who were brandishing a search warrant. Though he strenuously denied all knowledge of any smuggled goods, the evidence seemed to be against him when a cask of finest brandy was uncovered in the loft of his house. Triumphant, the officer sent his men to requisition a horse, while he himself made sure the evidence remained intact, by sitting on it.

William Arthur slipped his men a 'nod and a wink' and soon they were all making a great deal of noise all over the house. The Customs officer determinedly ignored it, telling himself that they were trying to distract him away from that precious cask of brandy. But what they were really doing, was boring a hole up through the floor and into the cask itself. The brandy had drained away long before the Customs men came back and it was discovered that the officer was sitting on an empty cask, all the vital evidence somehow vanished into thin air!

Chapter Fifteen
Cefnsidan and the Men of the Small Axes

Near Pembre on the eastern side of Carmarthen Bay, lie the sands of Cefnsidan. When a low tide is out, the skeletons of ancient ships become visible along this large expanse of smooth sand, half-buried, ravaged by the sea. For this beautiful spot is a sea cemetery — one of the most dangerous and treacherous places along the whole of the Welsh coast.

Traditionally, hundred of ships, large and small, have met their end on Cefnsidan sands. Only the names summon up the ghosts of those doomed vessels: *Esperance, Smiling Morn, Old Hunter, Britannia, Speedwell, Goodwill, Prairie Flower, Sarah Anne* and *Maid of Delos*. Many others which met their fate here have been forgotten.

In the old days, when the storm-clouds gathered and the winds gusted strongly from the south-west, ships would head for the Bristol Channel to shelter, only to be driven into Carmarthen Bay where their masters felt safer with the Pembrokeshire rocks looming to the west and the Gower Peninsula to the east. But they were now dangerously near the sands at Cefnsidan, and often the westerly wind would run these unsuspecting vessels aground, so that when the tide turned, they were left entrenched in their sandy graves. Sometimes too, the seas would be so savage that the ships would be broken up on the very sand itself, and crews would be swept away while cargoes were spread far and wide over the sands.

As in other parts of Wales, the people of Pembre and Pentwyn felt both compassion for the victims of the wrecks and a practical conviction that what the sea brought them, they were fully entitled to make the best use of. Not only cargoes were carried off, but ships were stripped of sails, ropes, timber. Mindful of the ready markets waiting in Carmarthen and Llanelli, the locals streamed across Cefnsidan sands with ponies and carts to carry away all that was moveable — and quite often, a great deal that was not. They carried small axes to cut away the planks and timbers of the stricken vessels, and became known as 'the Men of the Small Axes'.

The local landowners and gentry claimed that since they owned the seashore, they rightfully owned whatever the sea brought with it, and, in a similar manner to the disputes and court cases which arose elsewhere, they challenged the locals for their property. The Crown also claimed every wreck — but London was a long way from Cefnsidan at the beginning of the Nineteenth Century, and by the time authority arrived on the scene in the person of the appropriate officials, the 'Men of the Small Axes' had usually stripped the wreck in question bare.

On December 19, 1833, the *Brother*, en route from America to Liverpool carrying a cargo of 4000 buffalo hides and cotton, crashed on Cefnsidan sands. Only the ship's carpenter was rescued by a local man, the rest of the crew of 16 perished, and when the ship broke in half, the 'Men of the Small Axes' were waiting to retrieve the buffalo hides and bales of cotton. In addition, the Captain's gold watch and chain and a gold ring he had been wearing mysteriously disappeared.

The following day, a procession of ponies and carts could be seen crossing the sands, and the morning light glittered on the small axes as they were put to good use in cutting away the best timber. For two whole days, a small army of local people were busy helping themselves to whatever they could find, so that the large vessel was left as a mere skeleton.

Local Justice of the Peace J.H. Rees, who lived in Cilmaenllwyd Manor near Llanelli, was aware that the Crown was the rightful claimant of the wreck, and heard disturbing rumours that it was being looted. He took prompt action, saddling his horse and riding to the sands. On arrival, he shouted to the assembled crowds that they were breaking the law, but the 'Men of the Small Axes' — and their women too — simply laughed in his face and carried on with their plundering.

When he tried to assert his authority, a couple of the men brandished their axes menacingly, and, disconcerted, he retired to call the local constables, instructing them to guard the wreck. But the constables were too cowardly to stand in the way of these notorious men and their axes, and they refused, so that the looting continued unchecked.

In the end, the poor Justice of the Peace could do nothing except retire to his manor house, where he wrote a plaintive letter to the Home Office, which can be read today and brings the 'Men of the Small Axes' and their doings vividly to life:

> 'My Lord,
> . . . Carts have been sent from a distance of twenty miles round, to carry away the bales of cotton and timber of the vessel. . . the constables I had stationed along the sands which the goods were strewn. . . were unable to prevent them from carrying them off, and I was myself assaulted by two men. . .'
> Your Lordship's Obedient Humble Servant
>
> J.H. Rees.

Chapter Sixteen
The Business of Wrecks

After the drama, the rescues, the tragedies, of every wreck there is always a reaction. Around the coasts of Wales, we have seen that one of the main reactions of the local people over the centuries was to ensure that anything in the way of cargo or wreckage which might be useful to them was not allowed to slip through their fingers. And sometimes, there were disputes about cargoes or items which might have been washed ashore, indicating that even before the days when there were professional companies involved in the salvage business, competition in the making of money from wrecks could be fierce.

Among the papers of a solicitor from Beaumaris, who was active in the late 1700s, he many times mentions items cast up from wrecks over which there were fierce disputes. At Red Wharf in 1779, there was argument over 'several pieces of masts and yards' that had been washed ashore. Both the Bishops of Bangor and Vice-Admiral Hugh Owen, on whose behalf the solicitor was acting, laid claim to this valuable timber.

Various cannon and anchors were also energetically squabbled over, and the enterprising Thomas Williams of Llanidan — later to be known as the 'Copper King' because of his extensive business empire controlling the copper trade from his works at Parys Mountain on Anglesey — proved early on that he had an astute brain for recognising a good thing when he saw it. He appeared on the maritime scene in

Anglesey claiming he held 'a patent under the Prince of Wales' for the timber from a vessel that had been wrecked 'near Penrhos Villew' in October 1779, with the loss of all the crew.

Whether he did possess a patent or not, he not only stripped the vessel in question, but continued to seize timber and goods from other wrecks for his own use, in spite of storms of outrage directed at him from all sides. And not only did irregular seizure of cargoes and goods flourish, as we have seen, but either because they were involved, or because they turned a blind eye to the activities of others, the authorities often conveniently forgot to mention various items which were supposed to have survived a wreck, or dismissed them, saying for instance, 'a pipe of nasty wine not worth meddling with' or, as the Cefnamlwch agent wrote rather mysteriously on one occasion, 'a hogshead of brandy intirely concealed from me'.

It is worth repeating again that the most colourful stories and reports about cargoes which were lost, saved or squabbled over by the populace, the authorities and everyone else — as well as the most amusing — concerned wine, brandy or some other form of alcoholic beverage. Not for nothing did the smugglers who dared their way under the noses of the customs and revenue officers, make sure they smuggled plenty of wine as well as other luxury goods such as silks and tobacco. They knew that the average citizen would go far and pay well to buy their smuggled brandy.

It has been pointed out that the reaction of the local people towards a wrecked vessel might well have depended on the cargo it carried. Two ships were wrecked as a result of a terrible storm in December, 1847, for instance, and the newspaper reports concerning what happened to each of them could not have been more different. The *Frankfield*, outward bound from Liverpool to Cape Horn, came to grief on the shores of Anglesey, where 'scores of the good people of Cemaes were immediately on the beach' and the survivors were showered with assistance, kindness and every possible form of help.

In contrast, when the *Archduke Paladino*, laden with Indian corn and en route from Constantinople to Dublin, was wrecked in the same storm off Caernarfonshire, there was no account of assistance being rendered to the unfortunate crew. Instead, it was indignantly claimed that 'all work seems to be at a standstill, men, women and children have been fully engaged in robbing the vessel'.

When a few years earlier, the *Adelaide* was wrecked on Ynys Wellt,

Cymyran Bay, two hundred puncheons of brandy which she carried apparently disappeared there and then on the beach as they were washed ashore. It was recorded afterwards that large numbers of the local people were 'conveyed back to their dwellings in an insensible state in carts and on planks'.

Not surprisingly, in view of the number of flourishing non-conformist churches in Wales, there were two attitudes towards the smuggling of wines and brandies, and the eagerness to sample the cargo of a wrecked vessel if she happened to be carrying some similar sort of liquid refreshment. Many gave way all too willingly to temptation, while sterner temperance advocates regarded the brandy and the wine as probably responsible for every single thing that went wrong, including, on occasion, for the ship being wrecked in the first place.

The wreck of the *Brown*, on August 8, 1829 in Llanrhuddlad Bay came into this latter category, and the historian Aled Eames has recorded the hilarious tale of the wreck as it was detailed in a temperance pamphlet in the 1830s.

> 'On 8 August 1829,' he says, 'about 3 o'clock on a fine afternoon, the *Brown* had sailed from Dublin bound for Liverpool with a cargo of 50 cows, 39 sheep, 50 pigs, a crew of six, the wife of the Mate, and ten passengers. With much shaking of heads,. . . people read the story of the voyage: "Alas, instead of being thankful to God for fine weather, the seamen gave sacrifice to Satan in their favourite drink, Whisky," and with only an inexperienced youth on watch had found themselves in thick fog off the Anglesey coast with only a vague idea of their position. Shortly after two o'clock in the morning they struck a rock in Llanrhuddlad Bay. To add to the scandalised pamphleteer's horror, local people had flocked to the scene of a wreck at daybreak, some to help but many more to steal everything in sight, encouraging their children to do likewise, and this on the Sabbath morning. Alas for the church and chapel services that morning.'

It was only with the greatest reluctance that the coastal populace abandoned its drinking habits. Many were the occasions such as that which took place near Oxwich Point in 1940, when the Fisheries

Officer and Lloyds Agent for West Gower recorded that: 'Twenty odd casks came ashore on the Gower, seven of which were in my district. . . Two came in at Slade Cliff, and with horses, chains and men we hauled them up. When on the brink the chains slipped and the casks burst on the shingle. Men drank the stout (Guinness Dublin) from jam jars and flagons found hurriedly on the beach.'

It was even recollected by people who were on the scene, that some desperate souls got down on their hands and knees to lap up the precious liquor! And afterwards, there were bodies all over the beach. But no doubt those who had enjoyed their unexpected thirst-quenching considered it had been well worth the headaches they probably had on waking.

On another occasion, the local drinkers on this part of the coast were foiled when a crate of gin came ashore onto the sands. It was discovered by a party of nuns who were staying in a nearby hotel, and who dutifully handed it over to the authorities before it could be put to what the men would have considered its proper use!

In 1917, a cargo of French wine came ashore at Three Cliffs Bay on the Gower, and there were soon hundreds of people arriving armed with bottles, pans and jugs. Some had even brought buckets. But the result was the same as happened later in 1940 — the rising sun the next morning looked down on rows and rows of prone bodies, just opening their bleary eyes after having 'slept it off'.

In contrast to these stories of cargoes — whether in the possession of smugglers or due to the ship having been wrecked — being appropriated by the local people, is the tale of the *Bounty Hall*, an East Indiaman which came ashore in 1819 on Llanmadog Sands. By some miracle of fortune, she was undamaged, but since she was carrying a valuable cargo of sugar, spices and rice, the Swansea Cavalry set out immediately to protect it against the greedy fingers of the locals. When they arrived, however, they discovered that all the local people had done was to pile the cargo up tidily and then keep a watchful eye on it until it was claimed by the proper authority. What a wonderful sense of duty and community spirit!

As time passed, the business of shipping became less of a hit-and-miss affair. Marine insurance made certain that if there were wrecks, they would be covered so that the owners did not lose their entire fortunes. Summing up the romantic side of marine insurance is the story behind the famous Lutine Bell, which hangs in the underwriting rooms at Lloyds of London, and is popularly — though wrongly — believed to be rung whenever a ship goes down at sea.

The epitome of all stories of great treasure lost at sea, the bell originally belonged to *La Lutine*, a French frigate which, having been surrendered to the British in 1793 at Toulon, became *HMS Lutine*. She was carrying a cargo of gold and silver bullion to Hamburg in 1799, when she was caught in a terrible storm and was wrecked off the Dutch coast. All hands were lost, and her cargo — which has been valued as high as £1.4 million — was of course lost with her. The underwriters at Lloyds settled the insurance claim in full, and some of the bullion was later recovered, as well as items from the vessel herself, including the now famous bell. But Wales has had her own great treasure-ship tragedy, and we will hear about it in another chapter.

As well as being able to insure ships so that their loss did not mean bankruptcy, ship-owners were soon to become introduced to a new breed of men whose business lay with salvaging vessels lost at sea. In Anglesey, there were professional attempts at salvage as early as the 1840s, when a firm called the 'Brothers Jones, divers, of Hirael' successfully raised several vessels. There were other divers at work too. One from Bangor, referred to as Edwards, worked on the wreck of the *William Turner*, and reportedly raised chain, anchors, copper bolts and a gun.

One of the interesting features of long-gone wrecks today is what can be uncovered by modern divers who are not in the salvage business, or might not even be professional divers. The undersea explorers, members of sub-aqua clubs and others, are finding real treasure all around our shores — and Wales is no exception.

One of the most interesting wrecks which has been 'discovered' after lying forgotten on the sea bed, is that of the *Mary*, Britain's first Royal Yacht, which was originally presented to Charles II after his Restoration in 1660. Charles had sailed from Holland in a similar sort of Dutch-designed 'jaght', and declared he would not be satisfied until he had one of his own, so the Mayor of Amsterdam, Mr Van Vlooswyck, made haste to purchase the *Mary* from the Dutch East India Company and send her to Charles along with a smaller yacht, the *Bezan*.

It is recorded in the Diaries of Samuel Pepys how this gift introduced yacht racing to Britain, but by the time the *Mary* was wrecked in 1675, she had been sold to the Royal Navy. She was en route from Dublin to the Dee with several important passengers on board including the Earl of Meath and his son, when at about two o'clock in the morning, in foggy weather, she 'touched upon a rock to the N.W. of the Skerrys that lie to the Eastward of the bay of Holyhead'. At first, the sailors shouted reassuringly that all was well, but almost at once, the vessel struck another rock and sank almost immediately. Some of the crew and passengers managed to scramble to safety on the rocks, but thirty-five people, including the Earl of Meath, were drowned.

And there she lay in 40 feet of water, only to be accidentally discovered in 1971. Her ornate guns — some 5ft 11in long, cast in Amsterdam when the yacht was presented to Charles II in 1660 — have been brought to the surface along with smaller guns that were cast in the Tower of London and bear the cypher of Sir William Compton, Master of the Royal Ordnance from 1660 to 1663. Salvaging such items from a long-lost ship can truly be said to be a labour of love, and we owe a great deal to the divers and enthusiasts who spend their spare time investigating the world below our coastal waters and helping to make the secrets of our historic wrecks clearer to us.

Chapter Seventeen
A Treacherous Shore

The coast of Pembrokeshire has been described by historian Ted Goddard as 'one of the most dangerous stretches of coastline in the world'. He adds that: 'Pembrokeshire is at the crossroads of some of the busiest shipping routes and its waters are the graveyard of thousands of vessels caught in distress. From the earliest times, men and women have died on the county's treacherous shores.'

The records tell us that the local people indulged in as much smuggling, wrecking and scavenging when a vessel came to grief, as did the rest of the folk along the coasts of Wales. On December 17, 1668, for instance, when the *Amity* of Southampton was driven ashore near St David's Head, it was reported that 'the country people were so barbarous that they staved the wine casks in so much that the master saved not anything considerable, only some fruit which we indemnified. The officers of the Customs were there and could not find out one cask of wine.'

In January 1773, a notable wreck occurred near the entrance to Solva harbour, when the *Phoebe and Peggy* went down and over sixty lives were lost. Among them was a lady, whose fingers, so it was claimed, were broken when greedy hands grasped to steal her golden rings. A baby was also among the dead, and the story goes that the tiny body was stripped of its clothes by a pregnant woman when it was washed ashore. This inhuman act brought its own curse with it, however, for the woman died in childbirth, and her own baby died with her.

On the credit side, boats put out from Solva to try and effect a rescue, but as they were returning, more tragedy struck. One craft was lost in the heavy seas, and everyone on board perished.

As in other parts of Wales, there was much heroism and generosity along with the selfishness and greed that was evident whenever a wreck took place. When the *Oak* of Belfast was wrecked off Solva on October 17th, 1862, the survivors found, to their consternation, that their clothes had been stolen while they were recovering from their ordeal. James Nash, who recorded the details of many local wrecks in his notebooks, described how:

> 'Having clothed the boy (one of the survivors) with a suit of my own clothes, I had courage to ask the other [in the village] to give and glad I am to say they had plenty of clothes to give them, such as stockings, flannels, shirts, trousers, vests, also some money for each to have in his pockets.'

Along with justifiable pride that they generally met tragedy at sea with this same open-heartedness and in a spirit of giving all possible assistance to the survivors of a wreck, the people of Pembrokeshire displayed the traditional Welsh tendency to celebrate the more dramatic wrecks off their coast in song and story. One such was commemorated in the 'Ballad of Bitches Rock', composed after the drama was over by George Ashurst.

It happened on October 12th, 1910, when the ketch *Democrat*, which had been trying to shelter in Ramsey Sound, began to drag her anchors in the increasing gale, and signalled for assistance. In response, the St David's lifeboat, the *Gem*, was launched in the teeth of the gale and managed to take the master and crew of two off safely, even though both vessels were by now dangerously near the treacherous black rocks known as the Bitches. The lifeboat attempted to pull clear, but too late, and the coxwain made a desperate effort to avoid the rocks by taking the narrow passage through the reef, only recognisable by the boiling foam that marked it. As the vessel headed for safety, it hit a rock, and all on board were thrown into the swirling, tempest-tossed waves.

Fifteen survivors, including the crew of the *Democrat*, reached the Bitches, where they clung in perilous state. Three members of the lifeboat's crew, and the little ship herself, were swept away in the darkness and lost, while those who were clinging to their frail safety on the rocks only managed to attract attention when daylight came and they set fire to some oilskins.

The storm was still raging as fiercely as ever, and it seemed they had reached the sanctuary of the rocks only to perish. But under the leadership of a young fisherman called Sydney Mortimer, two coastguardmen went with him to Porthclais Harbour, across the headland, to launch a boat. It was the 20-foot *Wave Queen*, which soon ran into difficulties when, at the entrance to the Sound, a squall ripped away part of the rigging and almost swamped her. Not to be deterred, the heroic crew of three cut away the rest of the rigging, and Sydney Mortimer rowed with the steering lines fastened to his legs, while his crew baled.

Since it was impossible to approach the Bitches, the *Wave Queen* stood by for four hours until the tide fell enough for her to go near them. Five men were taken off safely and landed on Ramsey Island, and another five made the second trip. The *Wave Queen* was returning for a third rescue attempt when another boat arrived and rescued the remaining survivors. In addition, Fishguard's lifeboat had been alerted and had struggled through heavy seas for sixteen miles to assist. When she came on the scene, all the survivors had been rescued, but the second boat which had saved them from the Bitches was in difficulty, so the lifeboat was able to provide a tow to take her to safety. All the men were shaken, and some of the early survivors were in need of medical care.

It was hardly surprising that the RNLI as well as public donations paid tribute to those men who had died in this heroic rescue mission. Sydney Mortimer was awarded the RNLI's Silver Medal, and other awards were made to various members of the other crews.

But most lasting of all, possibly, is the ballad that immortalises this terrible night and these deeds of gallantry and high drama. This is how the 'Ballad of Bitches Rock' runs:

'The booming gun rang out its knell across the wave-swept bay;
'Twas midnight and midst the cottage homes sweet sleep held gentle
sway.
The sleepers woke, then bade farewell to sobbing babes and wives,
While spray and foam and shrieking wind screamed peril to their lives.

They reached the wreck and saved the crew, then turned to make for
port,
But now the sea, the baffled sea, with fury was distraught,
By mountain floods, she drove them back upon the Bitches Rock,
'Ha! Ha!,' she laughed in bitter scorn, 'Dar'st thou my rage to mock?'

The boat stove in upon the rocks, now swept by wind and tide,
And all essayed to save their lives by climbing up the side.
Drenched by the foam, they huddled close to stave off the flowing sea,
And thought of those they'd left at home across there on the lea.

Their oilskin coats they torches made, and shouted loud their plight,
But never answ'ring call came back, the wind laughed in its flight.
And death stared at them out the foam, and vainly tried to seize
Those stalwart sons so full of life, its hunger to appease.

And on the land their trembling wives searched for them through the
night,
And saw the flares that mournful beamed across the tempest's might.
Then dark despair came on the town and grief like mist o'erspread,
'No boat could live in such a sea,' experienced seamen said.

'Who'll join with me?' cried Mortimer, 'those billows wild to brave,
I cannot leave them to their fate without attempt to save.'
'We'll join with you,' the coastguard cried, 'We'll give a helping hand,
'Tis desperate, but we'll try our best to bring them to the land.'

Then daring men 'gainst Nature's might rowed out their little boat,
Husk, Guppy, Mortimer, the crew, those heroes' names to quote.
They dragged their comrades from the rocks and brought them safe to
shore,
To wailing wives, borne down with grief, their loved ones to restore.

My hand to you brave Mortimer! A lesson you have taught,
That courage, nobleness, is not alone with luxury wrought.
Amid the poor, the lowly born, they shine with brightest ray,
And show the glimmer of the soul embedded in its clay.'

It was a pity no-one ever thought to compose a ballad to celebrate the Pembrokeshire man who was awarded that most celebrated of all marks of honour for gallantry at sea, the RNLI Gold Medal. His name was John Howells, and he was coxwain of the Fishguard lifeboat *Charterhouse* when on December 3rd, 1920, that vessel was launched in response to signals of distress from the Dutch motor schooner *Hermina*, anchored off Fishguard.

By the time the lifeboat reached the *Hermina* she was in difficulties off the rocks, having dragged her anchors in the very heavy seas. It was almost impossible to get a line on board her, for the seas were so bad that the *Charterhouse* was at times being thrown up into the *Hermina*'s rigging and threatening to crash down onto the stricken ship's deck — but somehow Coxwain Howells managed it. He even got as far as taking seven of the crew off safely, but then came up against a snag. The Dutch captain, his chief officer and the second mate refused to leave their ship. Vainly, the Coxwain implored them to think again, warning them that under such terrible conditions, the lifeboat would not possibly be able to return, and that if they remained on board, they would be dashed to death as the *Hermina* was smashed against the crags at Needle Rock when the tide rose.

But they remained adamant, and, mindful of his duty to the other survivors and his own men, Coxwain Howells turned to return to Fishguard — only to discover that the lifeboat was now leaking! At first, the engine would not start — at length, it became obvious it was not going to start, and it was left to the Coxwain to abandon thoughts of returning home under the power of the engine, and to sail this much-tossed, battered and limping vessel against the horrific and too-close backdrop of ominously menacing cliffs to the safety of the harbour.

That, at least was the idea, but the vessel had no sooner started her terrible journey than the mizzen sail was ripped to shreds and disappeared into the dark, leaving only the mainsail. With the courageous leadership of their Coxwain in their minds as a shining example to follow, the second coxwain and one of the lifeboatmen went forward and, in the teeth of huge seas, managed to set the jib sail, an action which undoubtedly saved the vessel and everyone on board. The result was that, three hours after they had left the wreck — at the fateful hour of midnight — the heroic *Charterhouse* limped into Fishguard, her mission accomplished.

In fact, the three men who had been left behind on the *Hermina* signalled their distress some time later, and thanks to the dedication and skill of the crew manning the Rocket Apparatus on the cliff above Needle Rock, the lives of the Dutch captain and the chief officer were saved, though the third man was washed away and lost.

This was a rescue that was commemorated by awards to a large number of the lifeboat's crew, as well as the celebrated RNLI's Gold Medal to the coxwain. There were three Silver Medals and nine Bronze Medals in all awarded to the crew, as well as a 'monetary reward' for everyone. It was a proud moment for Pembrokeshire — indeed, for Wales — when the gallant lifeboatmen went to London in April 1921 to receive their awards.

And this was not the end. On the first anniversary of the rescue, the crew were presented with gold and silver watches by the Dutch Government and the Queen of the Netherlands. And, an elderly, retired man in his seventies, John Howells went back to London in 1924, to Buckingham Palace where he was presented with the Empire Gallantry Medal by King George V. His death in the following year, plunged the whole of sea-faring Wales into mourning.

So many were the wrecks which occurred over the years along the rocky coasts of Pembrokeshire, that the county can claim at least two 'ghost ships'. These, of course, were not really ghost ships at all, but abandoned vessels which refloated themselves and drifted away into the storm and the dark to meet their fate.

One was the *Sarah Macdonald*, which was wrecked on the Smalls on October 7th, 1911. The crew, who had scrambled to safety on the rocks, were taken off by the St David's Lifeboat, which then set out in hot pursuit of the 'ghost' vessel. Having managed to overhaul the errant ship, however, she was examined by the captain, who declared his vessel too badly damaged to save. So she was allowed to sink and the lifeboat returned with the living survivors to harbour.

The *Meridian*, en route from Par, in Cornwall, to Runcorn grounded near the Smalls in 1921, in foggy weather. The crew abandoned ship, but stood by for some seventeen hours, before they were rescued and taken to safety in Milford Haven. They assumed their ship had sunk, since they had long since lost sight of her, but in fact, she had sailed off into the fog after refloating, with not a soul on board. She proceeded to undertake an incredible solitary journey of nearly a hundred miles before she was wrecked — this time for good — on the coast of Ireland.

Pembrokeshire has had its share of wreckers and their nefarious activities too, but in one case the plunderers were visited with a deadly vengeance. The vessel in question was the merchantman *Increase*, which ran into trouble off the Pembrokeshire coast in January 1791. She was returning from St Kitts, in the Caribbean, with a cargo of 'condemned' gunpowder from the British garrison there, and when she went ashore at Druidston Haven, the local people assisted the survivors to leave the vessel when the tide went down, but proceeded to gather in large crowds the next morning ostensibly to help in rescue operations, but in reality to get their hands on anything they could, especially the liquor that was on board.

It was not long before the barrels of gunpowder — regardless of the fact that they were 'condemned' — were being tossed casually onto the rocks instead of being carefully thrown to seaward, and in addition, the locals decided they liked the look of the copper hoops that fastened the gunpowder barrels, and started to hack the casks of gunpowder open to take the copper, with the result that the powder was thrown far and wide over the rocks.

The tragedy that ensued was inevitable. Somehow, the gunpowder caught fire, and it is recorded that there were three terrible explosions, as a result of which over sixty people were burned. One woman was killed outright, and seven others died from their injuries within the next few days, while many — especially the women in their long, burning skirts — bore the marks of that ghastly morning until they died. The Rev. Moses Grant, Rector of Nolton Parish, insisted that:

> This calamity is plainly intended as a warning to desist from wreck plundering, for none were hurt on the side next to the sea, where the persons stood who were endeavouring to save (the cargo). . . May this be a warning on future occasions, for it had but little effect on the spot.'

Alas, one fears that the wreckers were too strong-stomached to let one tragedy discourage them, and as we have seen, bodies continued to be robbed of clothes, and dead fingers of their jewellery, in a long tradition among the coastal folk. Indeed, a young woman who visited the area after the wreck of the *Increase* recorded that in her view, the 'inhabitants of this rocky coast. . . experience nearly the same sensation at the sight of a ship labouring in a storm, as arises in the mind of an undertaker, when he contemplates the declining health of a wealthy citizen.' Fair comment, indeed!

Pembrokeshire has had, too, its share of multiple wrecks, one of the worst having taken place on November 10th, 1866. There were some eight ships in the Bristol Channel, attempting to make Milford Haven in a storm with torrential rain adding to the problem of the darkness so far as visibility was concerned. The first ship went aground in Mill Bay, and the others crashed into her in a terrifying 'pile-up' which sent the men in the lighthouse on St Ann's Head running onto the cliffs when they heard the splinter of vessels, and screams of the souls on board.

They were able to save fourteen seamen and eight others tried their luck in an open boat, landing safely at Dale. It was established later that of the vessels involved, the Rye barque *Commodore* had fared one of the best so far as the lives of the crews were concerned, since all her crew had been saved. So too had the crew of the schooner *King of the Forest* and the crews of the French smack *Alfred Eliza* and another vessel named the *Eliza and Jane*. Only the captain and one member of the crew of the schooner *Isobel* had escaped alive from the dreadful melee of ships and bodies on that dreadful storm-driven night, however, and they were badly battered. As for the rest of the vessels, it was impossible to identify them, and many of the dead whose bodies were recovered, and who were buried at Deal, were never identified at all, as their condition and the confusion of that awful night made the task beyond human skill. Just more nameless victims of so many wrecks over the centuries.

Another terrible disaster occurred in April 1943, when 72 officers and men aboard two landing craft, and six would-be rescuers died in gale-force winds and high seas as they too were running for Milford Haven. The crew of LCG 15 was dashed to pieces before the eyes of hundreds of horrified rescuers, as she went down between Sheep Island and Freshwater West, and those not dashed against the cruel rocks were drowned. LCG 16 went down during the night and though the St David's Lifeboat arrived in hazardous conditions — which were not helped by the knowledge that there were floating mines to contend with in the area as well as the awful state of the gale and the seas — the lifeboatmen found no-one and nothing except one man, badly injured and covered in oil. After a journey of eighteen miles to reach the disaster area (the Angle Lifeboat not being available as she was undergoing an overhaul) the crew of the St David's Lifeboat continued to search for survivors from one o'clock in the morning until daylight. When she finally returned home at 8.30 a.m. it was discovered there were two other survivors from the landing craft, who had been washed ashore. Three men out of a total of seventy-eight, including six who had tried to go to the rescue in the whaler of *HMS Rosemary*, an escort sloop which had attempted to give assistance. The whaler had been swamped within seconds of being launched. In the statement which was made in Parliament by the First Lord of the Admiralty, A.V. Alexander, it was stated that '. . . there is no question of the disaster being attributable to negligence.' This time, it was no-one's fault that the treacherous coast had claimed more wrecks!

Most of Pembrokeshire's historic wrecks are likely to be those of oil tankers, nowadays, since they come and go in large numbers to Milford Haven, and one wreck may require the assistance of many other vessels to deal with the damage and pollution the oil can cause. Sixty-six vessels were used when the *Christos Bitas* grounded some miles from the Smalls in October 1978, many in anti-pollution activities, since the tanker leaked an enormous oil slick which damaged wild life along the coast and killed nine thousand birds.

A good example of tragedy striking the oil tankers is the story of the first to arrive at the new Esso refinery terminal at Milford Haven in July 1960. She was the *Esso Portsmouth*, carrying 32,000 tons of crude oil from Kuwait. Berthed at the terminal, she caught fire at 6.30 a.m. on the morning of July 10th and there were three huge explosions which shook the whole port. The local Angle lifeboat was launched within minutes and tried to find survivors, standing by until the fire was got under control.

Fire-fighting tugs joined forces with the refinery firemen and the Pembrokeshire Fire Brigade, and though the chief steward died in the blaze and three other members of the crew were hurt, the rest of the people on board the *Esso Portsmouth* managed to escape. Some, including two women, jumped overboard and were picked up by rescue launches or else swam to safety. Fourteen more were taken safely off by the tug *Cassiope*.

This was not the end of the vessel's career as a wreck, however, for she was repaired, sold and renamed *Winston*. On route from Galveston to India she went aground in the South China Sea, and this time remained wrecked, since she was written off as a 'total loss'. The ill luck that had stalked her in Milford Haven had dogged her to the other side of the world.

Chapter Eighteen
The Wreck of the *Royal Charter*

On the night of October 25-26th, 1859, occurred what is probably the best known of all the wrecks off the Welsh coast, and possibly the worst — that of the 719-ton luxury steam clipper *Royal Charter*. Let us approach our account of her tragedy in the company of Charles Dickens, the Victorian novelist who visited the scene two months later in order to be able to describe it at first hand for the readers of his weekly magazine *All The Year Round*. Later he reprinted his account as the second chapter of his book *The Uncommercial Traveller*:

> 'Never had I seen a year going out, or going on, under quieter circumstances. Eighteen hundred and fifty-nine had but another day to live, and truly its end was Peace on that seashore that morning.
>
> 'So settled and orderly was everything seaward, in the bright light of the sun and under the transparent shadows of the clouds, that it was hard to imagine the bay otherwise for years past or to come, than it was that very day. The Tug-steamer lying a little off the shore, the Lighter lying still nearer to the shore, the boat alongside the Lighter, the regularly-turning windlass aboard the Lighter, the methodical figures at work, all slowly and regularly heaving up and down with the breathing of the sea, all seemed as much a part of the nature of the place as the tide itself. The tide

was on the flow, and had been for some two hours and a half; there was a slight obstruction in the sea within a few yards of my feet: as if the stump of a tree, with earth enough about it to keep it from lying horizontally on the water, had slipped a little from the land — and as I stood upon the beach and observed it dimpling the light swell that was coming in, I cast a stone over it.

'So orderly, so quiet, so regular — the rising and falling of the Tug-steamer, the Lighter, and the boat — the turning of the windlass — the coming in of the tide — that I myself seemed, to my own thinking, anything but new to the spot. Yet I had never seen it in my life a minute before, and had traversed two hundred miles to get at it.

'. . . O reader, haply turning this page by the fireside at home, and hearing the night wind rumble in the chimney, that slight obstruction was the uppermost fragment of the wreck of the *Royal Charter*, Australian trader and passenger ship, homeward bound, that struck here on the terrible morning of the twenty-sixth of this October, broke into three parts, went down with her treasure of at least five hundred human lives, and has never stirred since!

'From which point, or from which, she drove ashore, stern foremost; on which side, or on which, she passed the little island in the bay, for ages henceforth to be aground certain yards outside her; these are rendered bootless questions by the darkness of that night and the darkness of death. Here she went down.'

Culminating in two days of terror and destruction across the whole of Britain, the hurricane that struck on the 25-26th October, 1859 was fated to be known for ever afterwards as the *Royal Charter* gale, or the *Royal Charter* storm, in spite of the fact that hundreds of other vessels were lost during those fateful hours. A horrific total of 133 ships were sunk, while 90 were badly damaged. One schooner, the *Revival*, was amazingly wrecked before she had even been launched, being blown off her stocks at Porthdinllaen onto the beach.

Some 800 lives were lost during the hurricane's passing, which was twice as many than had perished at sea during the whole of the previous year, 1858. Ships were sliding uncontrollably in enormous crests of foam, while mountainous waves towered above them. Breakers crashed on the shore, and clouds of salt spray rose as though to reach the clouds in the grey lowering skies above and mingle into one. The whole earth shook terrifyingly.

There was a great deal of damage even inland. The hurricane struck first in the Channel, then along the coasts of Devon and Cornwall. Parts of the South Devon railway line were lifted and swept away, their protective embankments tossed aside by the gigantic seas and the winds, which in places were touching a hundred miles an hour. The waves drove in at a speed of 110 feet per second and mangled everything in their way into debris.

Ships which found themselves in distress were virtually done for, since it was impossible to launch any lifeboats or provide assistance of any sort. If you were caught in the hurricane, you were on your own and had to do the best you could — which in most cases, was just to hang on and hope you could stay afloat until the worst of the terror had passed.

It was 8 p.m. when the storm reached Anglesey — which was to be the setting for the wreck of the *Royal Charter*. By 10 that night, the full force of the hurricane was raging round the island and the early victims of the wind and waves were already meeting their fate.

One of the first to suffer was the huge iron paddle-steamer *Great Eastern*, which was outside Holyhead harbour. Alexander McKee tells us in his book *The Golden Wreck* that:

> 'inside the harbour, the masts of sunken vessels raised sheets of spray from the waves, while other ships, aground in the shallows, were rapidly being beaten into wrecks. In Penrhyn harbour, at Bangor, on the coast of North Wales, "the effect was truly appalling", wrote a witness. "The vessels were driven from one side of the harbour to the other in the greatest confusion; some were run into, and actually ridden over; others scuttled or dismasted, with their sides or their sterns ripped open, and their boats smashed." '

The strength of the wind, and consequent fury of the waves, is something difficult to comprehend. At Liverpool Observatory, a record wind force of 28 lbs to the square foot, something never previously known, was measured; the level of the sea rose four feet; and the speed of the gusts, many of them over 100 miles per hour, were beyond the measuring of the Beaufort Scale, whose Force 11, with winds up to 75 miles per hour and warnings of heavy damage if this rare and terrible situation should occur, was the highest previously noted. A normal gale could probably be counted on to measure Force 8 — but this storm was calculated to be Force 12, and there were no notes on how to deal with anything so drastic, or what might be expected to occur. This was, in fact, a unique occurrence, the hurricane of the century. And during the course of it, the *Royal Charter*, as well as all the other doomed vessels destined to suffer wreck or damage, went down off the Anglesey coast.

The story of the *Royal Charter* is a story of the Australian Gold Rush. She was a product of the demands for speed which were made by those who dealt in transporting both the seekers after gold and the gold itself, from Australia to Britain, and vice versa. The *Royal Charter* was a clipper ship, one of the fastest kinds of vessel to exist at that time, but she was made of iron, and she was also equipped with auxiliary steam power as well as sail.

Once gold had been discovered in Australia — £50,000 of it arriving in Liverpool in the *Albatross* in August, 1852 — there was no keeping up with the number of people who wanted to emigrate to the other side of the world to make their fortunes. Within the next five years, over 200,000 people had landed on the Australian coast. At least 4,000 of these were Welsh.

As with the journey to America, the voyage to the Antipodes was often horrific for the emigrants, particularly when, as often happened, the ships were becalmed, sometimes for weeks on end. Insanitary conditions — steerage passengers were often put on the lowest deck, even lower than the cattle which were travelling with the emigrants — meant that large numbers of people could and did die on their way to their destination. Up to a hundred deaths on a ship during one voyage was not uncommon.

As a result, the call was for faster ships which could somehow avoid the becalming that often lasted for weeks, when sails hung unmoving and the vessels were delayed. It was at these times on a voyage that disease was most likely to break out on board. The *Royal Charter* was one of the ships which were designed for speed, boasting the grace and elegance of the clipper with the usefulness of auxiliary steam, for those times when there was no wind to fill the sails. At the end of her maiden voyage, she achieved a new record and her owners were able to boast that in 'The magnificent steam clipper *Royal Charter*', passengers could reach 'Australia in under 60 days'.

In keeping with her terrible end which lay darkly in the future, however, the *Royal Charter*'s early days were dogged by bad luck — omens, some might have said, for tragedy to come.

She was a Welsh-built vessel, her birthplace being the Sandycroft iron-works on the River Dee in Flintshire, and when she was launched in 1855, the large crowd which had assembled to watch her slip — sideways, because the Dee was so narrow at this point that she could not be launched in the more usual fashion — into the water, watched in vein. At the moment of launching, the *Royal Charter* stayed put, and a trench had to be dug to assist her to float.

It had been hard work, but even while the diggers were resting after their toil, *Royal Charter* went aground on a sandbank near Flint while she was proceeding down the river, and was seriously damaged. Her main keel was bent, and she had to be taken to Liverpool to be repaired.

Even worse was to come when she was preparing for her maiden voyage, for since she was narrowly built, with very tall masts, it was believed that she might prove to be unstable, so large amounts of stone ballast were put into the hold, with the cargo on the top. It turned out that there was a great deal more cargo than had been anticipated, so by the time all had been stowed, the weight of it meant the ship's main deck was a mere six feet above the waterline.

In this condition, practically swamped, she set out from Liverpool to Australia on January 18th, 1856, and soon discovered that the hundreds of tons of ballast had been an awful error — not only did she not need it but it was cramping her style, making her drag her screw so that the propeller shaft almost broke. A week out, in a gale off Finisterre, the situation became so desperate that the Captain was considering returning to England, in spite of the disastrous effect this would have on the ship's and her owners' reputation. As well as having difficulty with the machinery, he was aware that water was slopping over the sides of the vessel, and that the lower decks were awash with it, soaking everything including the passengers in the third class and their belongings.

Nothing could be done until the hundreds of tons of ballast were removed, which necessitated the ship returning to harbour — so Captain Boyce turned about and headed for Plymouth, steaming into

Plymouth Sound on January 26th. The ballast was unloaded and the ship was made ready to sail once again — and on February 16th, she set off once more, this time on the triumphant record-breaking run which was to take her to Melbourne in under sixty days.

By the year 1859, the *Royal Charter* was a noted and indeed famous ship. She was luxurious and comfortable, fast, prompt, an asset to her owners. And in August, 1859, she prepared to sail from Melbourne with more than just her usual quota of passengers and cargo aboard. As she lay in the roadstead at Melbourne, a small steamer containing square wooden boxes came alongside, and the boxes, each checked personally by the Captain and an Australian customs officer, were handed aboard to be stored in the strongroom, which lay at the stern of the vessel, deep within the hull.

Each box was marked significantly with its weight and the name of the shipper, also with the name of the bank for which it was being consigned. For these boxes contained the treasure for which so many hopeful emigrants had made the passage to Australia — gold, then valued at £4 per ounce.

They had been secured in the banks ashore after they had been weighed, and brought to the ship under a police escort. They were heavily guarded every step of the way from the banks to the security of the strongroom. And when they were finally loaded, the Captain handed over a receipt for the staggering sum of £322,440. So on her voyage to England, the *Royal Charter* would be sailing as a treasure ship in the truest sense.

In fact, there was more treasure aboard than the Captain's receipt guaranteed, for many of the passengers were carrying their own personal fortunes with them in money-belts or among their luggage. James Dean, a smith who had gone out from England to make his fortune, had been lucky at the gold diggings. He carried with him a cheque on an English bank for a considerable amount of money, safely stowed in a waterproof belt he wore round his waist.

Mrs S.A. Foster, owner of the Shakespeare Hotel, Manchester, had been forced to travel to Australia to consult with her husband, who was busy establishing new hotels in the Antipodes. As a result, Mrs Foster was returning to England with almost £5,000 in money and valuables in her possession. These were only two of the many other passengers who were coming home to England richer than when they had left it.

On August 26th, 1859, the *Royal Charter* sailed from Melbourne with approximately 390 passengers on board. Her Captain was Thomas Taylor, who had been with her on her maiden voyage as a passenger, and who, by all accounts, was a rough diamond of a man who had risen from the ranks on his own merit, but who was an excellent commander and seaman. He was strict, he was proud, but he had reason to be — he was the commander of the *Royal Charter*, and he ran her well.

The vessel completed a full two months of her journey, sailing non-stop round Cape Horn and sighting the southern coast of Ireland on October 24th. Here she stopped to allow passengers ashore at Queenstown, and many of those remaining on board wrote letters to be posted on shore, letting their families and friends know that they were almost at the end of their journey.

In view of what was to happen to the *Royal Charter* only a few days later, these letters make tragic and touching reading.

A young midshipman, Frederick Foster, dashed off:

'We are now coming up the Channel with a slashing breeze. We ran out in fifty-nine days, and should have come home in forty-seven, had we not had strong head winds all the way from the line. You may expect me and one or two friends at your house Tuesday or Wednesday night, so be prepared. How is Alice? Remember me kindly to her and all. Excuse bad writing.'

Frederick Foster was to perish in the wreck.

Another passenger who was to die, Joseph Robinson, was busy making plans for his return. His sister Isabella was to make 'a good apple cake, and we must have tea by ourselves. . . and Isabella, you must come down to meet the night train, and stand in front of the ladies' waiting room. In order that you may know me, for I am much changed in my appearance since I left, I will call the word 'Brown'.' We can only visualise poor Isabella waiting and waiting in vain for the brother who would never return home again.

On the evening of October 24th, the passengers, in high spirits, presented a testimonial to Captain Taylor, to show their appreciation for the ship and for the fast voyage they had had so far. The Captain, in return, promised them that they would be in Liverpool within twenty-four hours. His words were later to ring ominously when applied to what happened to the ship, which of course never did reach Liverpool.

It was during the morning of the following day, Tuesday, October 25th, that the weather began to worsen. The ship was off the coast of Caernarfonshire when the wind freshened, and the sails were taken in. But by 1.30 in the afternoon, when the *Royal Charter* was passing Holyhead island there was still little sign of the hurricane that was sweeping its way up from the south. The sea was calm, though hazy fog lay inland. It was declared afterwards that one of the passengers who was a ship's captain had said they were in for a 'dirty night', but in spite of a rather strange appearance about the weather, which nobody could really explain, not even the barometers — of which the *Royal Charter* carried three — so much as hinted that anything out of the ordinary was about to break and hit the vessel.

Most of the passengers, particularly those who had sent letters from Queenstown, were looking forward to being reunited with their families and loved ones on the quayside at Liverpool. They had travelled so far, and now they were so near, so very near to home.

At 4.30 in the afternoon, the vessel passed the harbour at Holyhead, and there was some excitement amongst the passengers at the sight of the enormous *Great Eastern* lurking outside the breakwater, too huge to enter the harbour. Some of them went up on deck to view the monster steamship as the *Royal Charter* sailed past and on round the coast of Anglesey. And soon afterwards, the winds of the hurricane broke in all their fury upon the whole coastline, on Holyhead harbour, and on the *Royal Charter* out at sea.

A Special Correspondent for the 'Times', who happened to be in the area stayed up all night to make notes on what happened. He wrote:

'The wind gradually freshened during the afternoon, though not very much, till over the mountain came a thin black haze, which rose into the air with ominous rapidity and overspread the sky. The sea and wind kept rising as the glass fell, and before eight it blew a heavy gale from the eastward, with fierce squalls and storms of rain. As night wore on, the wind increased and came in fearful gusts, tearing away among the spars and rigging with a hoarse sustained roar that was awful to listen to, especially when one bore in mind that the glass was still falling, and that what we saw was only the commencement of the gale.'

113

What it actually felt like to be at sea when the gale was at its height, nobody who experienced this horrific phenomenon was ever able to describe afterwards with any coherency. The event was beyond description, the shambles, the pain and the anguish which those who were to suffer the full fury of the hurricane suffered.

Captain Taylor had the choice when the weather worsened, of running to Holyhead for shelter while the storm passed, or attempting to make Liverpool. He decided to keep on rather than delay the voyage, since he felt the reputation of making it from Melbourne to Liverpool in 'under 60 days' was at stake, and also he personally had promised his first class passengers only a short time ago when they presented him with his testimonial just out of Queenstown, that he would get them to Liverpool within twenty-four hours. His pride and the pride of the ship was, he felt, at stake.

There was a good seventy miles remaining to sail but with a little luck, the ship could still reach Liverpool within the twenty-four hours — and the 'under 60 days' — that had been promised. And in addition, the Captain had no idea of the danger in which his ship stood. There was nothing to warn him that the hurricane which was gathering force about to break over the *Royal Charter* was far worse than anything the ship had ever experienced or encountered. She had withstood many gales and hurricanes in the past, and once she had rounded Anglesey, she would be relatively sheltered and able to run eastward before the wind, straight for Liverpool.

Alexander McKee describes graphically how:

> '. . . the clipper drove on, under the beat of her engine, lights blazing along her sides, indicative of the warmth within, while the cold wind roared through her rigging and the giant waves came riding out of the murk to the eastward. Her motion was not uneasy, for she rode the waves buoyantly; her passengers were not alarmed, although some, no doubt, were seasick. They all had perfect confidence in the ship and her Captain. Captain Taylor, for his part, intended to pick up the pilot-boat which patrolled north of Anglesey, off Point Lynas, where the lighthouse was. He, too, had no premonition, and did not come on deck until some hours later.'

By six o'clock in the evening, when the ship had rounded the

Skerries and was turning in a wide sweep eastwards into Liverpool Bay, the temper of the storm and the winds had changed. In the gathering darkness, there were new notes of eldritch shrieking in the rigging, and signs that the hurricane was not far away — blown spray, white crests on the waves, and the wind increasing its strength. Yet still these signs gave no real indication of what was to come, nor any warning to the Captain of the *Royal Charter*.

Because of the nature of the hurricane, the winds it brought kept turning in a circle, so that a seaman's usual ability to count on his knowledge of the winds and how they might veer and change, was less than useless. As a result of this, the *Royal Charter* found herself about to be driven onto the Anglesey shore, with no searoom to maoevre and nowhere to run. At about half past six in the evening, she sent off rockets and fired guns in a signal for a pilot. She was to continue firing signal guns and rockets as the situation worsened, and showing a blue light to ask for assistance, but the tragedy was that though there were two Liverpool Pilot Boats, Nos 4 and 11, somewhere in the vicinity — a member of the crew of Pilot Boat No. 11 even saw her signals of distress and reported them to the master, who was able to view the blue light himself — there was nothing whatsoever that they could do to help. The weather now was so bad that even if they had been able to reach the vessel, they could never have boarded her.

Both Pilot Boats were driven hither and thither, tossed about like matchsticks, as the crews tried to save themselves and ride out the terrible storm. Likewise, the coxwain of the Moelfre lifeboat, out that night in his small fishing smack, was only a few miles from the *Royal Charter*, but he was not aware of sight nor sound of her distress signals, and even if he had been, there was nothing he could have done for her. He himself managed to get safely ashore at Moelfre round about midnight, but he and his colleagues rightly refused to take the lifeboat out, since they would have been condemning the crew to certain death, such was the violence of the gale.

Aboard the *Royal Charter* the Captain's efforts to control her had resulted in a situation where she would not answer her rudder and was being driven by the wind. Round about 10 p.m., it was evident that she was drifting towards the shore, a situation fraught with disaster, so the Captain gave the order 'Prepare to let go anchors!'

The screaming of the wind and the terrible rain-lashed gale was so bad that it was barely possible to see or hear anything even in the immediate vicinity, but the Captain — after trying vainly to turn the ship so that she could run into the Irish Sea rather than remain on her present course towards the rocky coast of Anglesey — ordered the port anchor let go at about 11 p.m. It was hoped that the weight of the anchor chain would steady the ship and stop her drift towards the rocks of the coast. When she continued to drift, the starboard anchor too was let go. The *Royal Charter*, held only by the weight of those massive fathoms of anchor chain, seemed steadier and the tension aboard, in Captain, crew and passengers, relaxed somewhat, though the situation was still desperate.

In the meantime, one ship had already come to grief on this part of the coast, but she was relatively lucky. She was the brigantine *Maria*, which was tossed like a piece of matchwood towards the shore and was thrown, not onto the rocks of Moelfre or the dangerous cliffs at Benllech, but onto the sands at Red Wharf Bay, stranded amid the streaming waves. The survivors climbed the rigging and waited for dawn — or rescue — whichever should come first.

The *Great Eastern*, too was in difficulties outside Holyhead harbour. 'One by one,' says Alexander McKee, 'her saloon skylights were blown in, and a deluge of driven rain and spray poured down onto the expensive carpets and furnishings, reducing them to a soggy mess. It was impossible to stand on deck, in the violent gusts, except by holding on. The great ship was steaming to her anchors, the screw going in order to ease the strain on the tortured iron cables. Inside the breakwater, the masts of a vessel which had sunk at anchor raised spouts of spray at every passing roller as it went racing for the shore; four ships lay aground in the shallows, pounding on the seabed, their sails torn out into tattered ribands by the 100-mile-an-hour winds. Those vessels still afloat in the harbour seemed hardly better off, plunging their battered bows deep under with every wave.'

As he had been reluctant to fail to keep his promise that they would be in Liverpool within twenty-four hours, so Captain Taylor, bearing in mind the complete confidence his passengers had in his ability even in this obviously unnerving situation, was reluctant to admit that the ship was in any real danger. He told some of the passengers who were sitting up late waiting for some reassurance that it was safe to go to their cabins, that he had the ship 'fast by the nose', and dismissed suggestions that the masts should be cut away. Some time later, at 1.30 a.m., he was once more reassuring the passengers — particularly the ladies — who were still up, and ordering coffee for all of them, when tragedy struck. The port cable broke, and the Captain went on deck to cope with this desperate situation.

He ordered the stream anchor to be brought up from the orlop, and more cable on the starboard anchor. There was much debating as to whether it would be wiser to cut away the masts so that the strain on the anchor cable would be lessened, but Captain Taylor decided to leave the masts intact and trust to the anchor cable and the screw of the ship, which was threshing frantically, trying to keep the ship stable against the gale.

And then, at about 2.30 a.m., final disaster struck the *Royal Charter*. The starboard anchor cable parted and the ship heeled, turned and drove before the hurricane winds straight for the land that lay invisible in the black night ahead. Like sections of film, frozen into slow motion, incidents and scenes flash before our eyes as they do in any disaster or tragedy. The boatswain's mate, who was standing near the wheel, called out asking whether the rigging should be cut away, and the Captain replied: 'Not yet, my boy'.

Distress guns exploded into the night, and rockets lit up the sky. All the signals asking for assistance were displayed throughout the length and breadth of the ship — but there was no-one to see or hear them, and even if there had been any observers, they would have been powerless to help.

About 3 o'clock, in desperation and in a last effort to try and save his ship, the Captain did order the masts to be cut away. Meantime, the passengers were roused and for the first time, told that they might be in deadly danger. Their panic and terror did not help matters. One of the passengers, Thomas Grundy, later described the interior of the saloon, where the passengers were being herded together to keep them out of danger when the mast fell.

'It was crowded with ladies and gentlemen in the utmost state of tremor. Families were all clinging to each other; children were crying out piteously, whilst parents were endeavouring to soothe them with cheering hopes.'

The *Royal Charter* had struck, and the evidence was that she shuddered and thumped, while tremors shook her frame beneath the passengers' feet. But so far, she had not been holed, or ripped open.

The Captain sent an apprentice boy down to reassure those crowded below decks and to tell those on deck, that everything was all right, they had struck a sandbank. But the boy's words did not carry conviction.

Edward Wilson, an Able Seaman, described what was happening as: 'Nothing but confusion on deck, fore and aft passengers, saloon, cabin and steerage all mixed together, fathers and mothers clasping their children in their arms, wives clinging to their husbands, shrieking, and crying, 'Save me, save me', 'Don't leave me', and so on.'

Eventually the Captain himself appeared looking cool and in control. 'Now, ladies,' he declared, 'you need not be at all afraid. We are on a sandy beach, and embedded in the sand. We are not ten paces from the shore, and the tide will leave us dry, and in ten minutes you will all be safe.'

This had the desired effect, and the passengers began to prepare themselves for going ashore. But in fact, the situation was not quite so simple as the Captain had described. The ship was indeed aground on a sandy beach, but she had been driven sideways on by the terrifying waves. And the tide, now on the turn, was not about to go out leaving the ship exposed so that the passengers could walk ashore, as the Captain thought. In fact, the tide was about to come in and the raging waters were to provide the death-blow for those aboard the *Royal Charter*.

The ship continued to signal its distress rockets and guns while the masts were hacked away, toppling over the sides. One heavy yard hit the deck as it fell, and through the broken deckhead, the waves tossed foaming water in onto the terrified passengers. The waves pounding against the ship made it stagger, and the passengers found it difficult to keep their footing. They were understandably in great fear, in spite of the Captain's promise that they would soon be ashore.

But when at last the dawn came after what had seemed an endless night, when at last the Captain, crew and passengers could see where they were, they could hardly believe their eyes. For they were aground a mere twenty-five yards from the land. This short distance was all that separated them from the rocks and headland which, wild and forbidding, loomed before them. But between the ship and the tumbled layers of rock, the waves thundered in a terrifying manner, so that it seemed impossible to bridge the gap between life on the coast, where there were men already looking out at the spectacle of the doomed ship, and the fate that awaited them where they were.

No sooner had the light revealed the awful situation of the *Royal Charter*, beating impotently in the grip of huge waves up to sixty feet high, than there were men from Moelfre gathering on the cliffs ready and willing to give any assistance they could, but unable for the moment to do anything.

On board, the obvious course of action seemed to be to get a line ashore and rig up a bosun's chair by means of which those on the ship could reach safety. A Maltese seaman, Joseph Rogers, immediately volunteered, and without further ado, let himself down into the maelstrom of seething water between ship and shore. Other seamen who had also volunteered were less courageous, and never actually made the attempt. While they were trying to pluck up their courage, delaying the moment when they must dare those terrible seas, Joseph Rogers managed to reach the shore and was dragged to safety by the rapidly increasing crowd of villagers on the cliffs. With this swim — of less than thirty yards — Joseph Rogers had earned himself a place in history.

While Rogers, exhausted and freezing from his ordeal, was taken to a nearby cottage to recover, frantic attempts were made to rig up the bosun's chair which would be able to transport the passengers from the ship to the shore. But the prospect was an alarming one. The *Royal Charter* was currently being driven nearer and nearer to the rocks by the heavy seas and huge waves, and anybody who had the courage to try and reach safety by means of the bosun's chair would be battered and drenched for most of the journey in the high wave crests. It was not something to undertake lightly, though if the passengers had been aware just how grave was their plight, and how great their danger, they would probably not have hesitated. As it was, one young woman became hysterical when attempts were made to coax her to take her place within in and be hauled to safety. She held up the evacuation of the passengers for at least ten minutes, adamantly refusing. When she would not go, some members of the crew scrambled forward, eager to take their turn, and once safely ashore, they assisted with the rescue party on the shore. But for most of those aboard the *Royal Charter*, it was too late.

The breakers had continued to pound the vessel upon the sand where she was aground, and drive her inland. Close to her hull, but not visible from above, was a fantastic jumble of stony ledges and rocks, and at some time between 6.30 and 7 a.m., the ship gave a great lurch and hit those rocks. She snapped in two, and gigantic waves washed through her from stem to stern, taking the screaming passengers with them.

Many were crushed between the two pieces of the ship, others were battered in the waves. Some were thrown ashore. And those who remained aboard the stricken vessel stood petrified, too shocked by what had happened to move or try to help themselves.

Again we turn to the account of the saloon passenger Thomas Grundy, who described the moment when the ship struck:

> 'A great sea came against the broadside, and divided the ship in two, just at the engine house, as one would smash a pipe stem, and the sea washed quite through her. People were carried down by the debris, and as many must have been killed as drowned.'

Another passenger, James Russell, together with his wife and two little girls aged ten and two-and-a-half, was on the point of going up on deck, and they clung to the rail at the top of the stairs. James Russell recorded afterwards:

> 'We found we were on the stern part of the vessel, separated from the fore part by a yawning chasm, into which every moment human beings were dropping, or being driven by the waves.'

One member of the crew who went down with the debris and was badly injured, but was later tossed ashore alive, recollected his last glimpse of the ship before he fell:

> '. . . three little children, standing on deck, holding each other's hands, screaming.'

A steerage passenger, John Judge, was washed out of the ship from below decks, by the great seas that ran through her. He said later:

> I saw hundreds of people closed up in the jaws of death around me.'

Mostly, those who had so far survived had been on the upper deck; people below would have stood no chance at all. And many had fallen into the boiling turmoil of water between the ship and the shore. There were arms everywhere desperately reaching out trying to clutch at help, and half-smothered screams which the seas choked away. In addition to the people struggling to remain afloat, the water was littered with fallen debris of all kinds, and even more terrible, with the mangled bodies of those who had been battered to death by the heavy debris against the rocks. Horribly mutilated, they mingled with the living, as did the torn-off limbs, and even heads, which the vicious seas had dashed away.

The scene was ghastly in the extreme, and was all the more terrible since most of the people who died did so because of the heavy and voluminous clothes they were wearing. The waves threw them ashore, but the weight of their sodden clothes — and also, significantly, the money-belts and heavy cash that many of them had tried to save — either sent them to the bottom immediately, or prevented them from being able to stand or get out of the water. So the waves drew them back remorselessly and implacably.

Not all of the passengers had been tossed into the water when the ship broke, and in the stern section, in the saloon, were most of the women and children. Separated now as they were by the foaming waters, from the bow section where the bosun's chair was still able to ferry those lucky members of the crew who could make use of it ashore, they were not able to be saved.

One crew member whose fate marked the most amazing coincidence was a young sailor called Isaac Lewis. He was a Moelfre man, and while he was taking his turn waiting to sit in the bosun's chair, he was close enough to the cliffs to recognise his own father's face among the crowds of rescuers on the shore. Dramatically, he is supposed to have cried out to his father — who likewise recognised his son — 'Oh, I am come home to die!' And either because he was swept from the bosun's chair by a huge wave, or because he managed to reach the cliffs only to be dragged back by the sea, he did not survive. His body was washed up less than a mile from his home later that day.

Now that the ship had split in two, each half was being pounded unmercifully in the terrible seas, and it was not long before they broke up completely. All who were left aboard were swept into the maw of the deep. Edward Wilson, one of the seamen who later reached the shore safely, was watching in horror and reported:

'It was dreadful, dreadful. There were mangled bodies floating about in the water; men, women and children standing up on the deck and shrieking for assistance; others on their knees, praying; others being washed overboard. There was a large number of passengers huddled on deck to the end; the shrieks of the poor creatures as they met their death was absolutely appalling.'

In the chilling space of a few moments, the *Royal Charter* met her end and nothing was left of the great vessel but the stumps where her masts had been cut away protruding from the seas.

The bravery of the villagers — particularly a group of them who were known later as 'the twenty-eight' and who had carried out the rescues at the risk of their own lives — was incredible during these terrible hours. One man alone would have been swept away if he had tried to save the sodden bodies as they were washed ashore, but the men of Moelfre linked hands to form a human chain, and dared the violence of the enormous waves time after time, in their unceasing efforts to save any who were thrown within their reach. The hurricane showed no sign of abating, and it was a measure of the fury and strength of the waves that a piece of ironwork from the ship's side, picked up later when salvage operations were being carried out, had a solid gold ingot and several gold coins embedded into it, as though the iron had been liquid when the softer gold was driven in. The seas had done that.

The Captain perished with his ship. He had been hurled across the deck by one enormous wave, and as he tried to struggle to his feet, thrown by another against the side of the companionway. He was for some time entangled in the wreckage of woodwork, and lay there, we are told, 'exposed to every wave that broke over the ship.' Even when released, he must have been dazed and disorientated. Just before the final break-up occurred, he and some members of the crew tried to lower a boat — which was to be immediately smashed to nothing — and he said to the few remaining passengers: 'The *Royal Charter* is all right; you will soon be saved.' His own end came only a few moments later.

Out of the total number of people who had been on board the *Royal Charter* — and since the passenger lists vary, the figure could have been anything between 472 and 498 — the survivors numbered only forty, comprising twenty-two passengers and eighteen crew. All of them were men. Not a single woman or child lived through their dreadful ordeal; and all the officers died.

Most of the survivors had come ashore nearly naked, such was the drag and pull of the water that their clothes had been ripped off. Fortified in warm clothing and whatever else the villagers could give them, they began to take stock and look round at each other and at the mangled remains of their fellow-travellers. In the aftermath of the wreck itself, there were scenes of terrible anguish and grief.

One passenger, James Russell, discovered amongst the bodies, the remains of his eldest daughter who had been torn from him by the waves along with her mother and her little sister. Observers wrote:

'It was a heartrending sight to witness that bereaved father carrying in his arms his dead off-spring up the rocky heights to Moelfre. We saw the little innocent in one of the cottages, carefully wrapped in a white sheet; it looked as if sleeping peacefully.'

A thought that was even more unbearable to contemplate when the events which had led to the wreck became clear, was the fact that the tragedy could so easily have been averted, or at least, alleviated to some extent. If the ship had struck a mere two hundred yards to the east, or if the passengers could have tried to swim in that direction, there was a little shingle beach, a haven when compared to the cruel rocks which had taken so many lives. It seemed to the public at large, when news of the tragedy spread the length and breadth of the country, that there had to be some reason for the loss of this great ship; someone had to be blamed.

The obvious person to shoulder the blame appeared to be the Captain, and rumours began to circulate that the Captain had been drunk, that he had failed in his duty. There was a great deal of strong feeling on the subject, as those who had lost loved ones tried to come to terms with their grief. But at the Inquest, which was held in the school building near Llanallgo Church, the verdict reached by the jury was that the loss of the *Royal Charter* had been purely an accident, that the Captain had been 'perfectly sober' and that he had done 'all in his power' to save the ship and the people on board.

Charles Dickens recorded what the rector of Llanallgo Church, where the dead had been brought for identification after the tragedy, said about another very thorny subject which scandalised the whole of the country:

'(The people of Moelfre) had done very well, and had assisted readily. Ten shillings had been paid for the bringing of each body up to the church, but the way was steep, and a horse and cart (in which it was wrapped in a sheet) were necessary, and three or four men, and all things considered, it was not a great price. The people were none the richer for the wreck. . .'

This would seem to give the lie to the rumours that went round, horrifying all who heard them, that the people of Moelfre had enriched themselves at the expense of not only the ship's cargo and fittings and whatever else might float in on the tide, but the precious gold in the strongroom and — worst of all — the very bodies of the victims as they came ashore. Commander M'Gregor of the Anglesey Coast Guard telegraphed an urgent message to Liverpool asking for assistance, declaring: 'The inhabitants of the district are stripping and plundering the bodies to a shocking extent.'

The local Coastguards, the Militia from Beaumaris and an Army detachment from Chester swelled the ranks of coastguardmen and thirty Marines, who took charge of the situation, in particular the recovery of the gold, whether it was in the form of scattered coins which were washed up by the sea, or the boxes which had been in the strongroom. It was officially declared after three months' salvage work on the wreck, that all the consignment of bullion except £30,000 had been recovered by the salvage team.

In spite of the Reverend Stephen Roose Hughes' insistence that none of the villagers benefitted from the wreck, we can be reasonably certain that, with their intimate knowledge of the coast and the seas of the area, their awareness of where wreckage might come ashore, even if miles from the scene of the wreck, enough of the treasure made its way into the pockets of the local inhabitants to ensure that most of them would never want again.

But as in all times of tragedy, heroism went side by side with greed. Many of the villagers were concerned with nothing except doing all they could, and more, not only for the shocked and injured living, but for the terribly mutilated dead. The bodies were laid in the church, and some in the cottages of the villagers. Relatives and mourners hurried from all parts of the country to this remote spot, desperate to find their loves ones — or, if it had to be, the bodies of their loved ones. Huge crowds of distraught brothers, sisters, parents, came thronging into Moelfre along the narrow and uncomfortable road from the mainland.

Even more heart-breaking to deal with were the letters which were sent hopefully, asking if a loved one could be identified. It became the sad task of the rector, the Reverend Stephen Roose Hughes, to reply to them. But how was he to identify a mangled corpse as a brother who had had 'bright grey eyes and a pleasant smile'?

Many of the mourners seeking their dear ones found the scene in the church unbearable, and the rector and his wife got into the habit of asking relatives who had arrived for details, and making a search among the still figures lying in rows, themselves. If they thought they had found the person who was being sought, they would take the mourners in blindfolded, and only take the blindfold away when they had reached the body in question. But even this was too much for some of the visitors, who collapsed with shock at the horrific sights that met their eyes.

The rector was a gentle, courageous victim of the wreck himself, for in his efforts to provide comfort and solace to the mourners and the bereaved, he not only undertook the physical task of upholding them as they walked into his church to collapse sobbing, overcome, but he replied to every letter that was written asking for information or comfort at the loss of loved ones. In all, he wrote 1075 letters, every one filled with compassion and emotional strength. To many of the bereaved, he must have seemed like a rock to which they could cling. But his own strength was limited, and he died only two years later, worn out by the terrible burden that had been placed upon his shoulders.

At the Inquiry for the Board of Trade, which opened in Liverpool on November 15th, some of the sad facts which marked the loss of this ship as particularly distressing were brought to light. This was not the most terrible wreck of the era — there had been others of similar magnitude — but what made this so appalling was the fact that the ship had sailed 16,000 miles, and been lost within only a few miles from her destination, within sight, within touching distance almost, of the shore.

By the end of the Inquiry, the court was satisfied that the ship had been perfectly seaworthy, and the Captain and officers had done all their duty demanded to try and save the ship and those aboard her. The fact that she lay in three pieces on the rocky bottom, that most of her passengers and crew had been battered to death against those same rocks, and that her owners were now bankrupt — nobody was responsible for this sad state of affairs. It had happened by pure mischance, Act of God, call it what you will.

And now all that remains of that terrible day is the wreck itself, which still lies off the Anglesey coast in some 18 feet of water; and a memorial stone erected in Llanallgo churchyard to those who perished. On the many graves which had to be dug for the victims, time has now sown grasses and flowers, and dimmed the suffering and the anguish. We can only hope they are at rest.

Chapter Nineteen
A Hundred Years Later

One hundred years and a day — or, give or take a few hours, exactly one hundred years — after the wreck of the *Royal Charter*, a more modern vessel was also wrecked in a hurricane in exactly the same bay, as though to drive the coincidence of this sad anniversary home to all who heard the tale.

The date was October 27th, 1959. The ship in question was the 650-ton steamer *Hindlea*, and it must have come as a sad and bitter echo from the past to the coxwain of the Moelfre lifeboat, Richard Evans, when only the day after a special service had been held at Llanallgo Church to commemorate the sinking of the *Royal Charter*, he received a telephone message that a coaster sheltering in Dulas Bay had started to drag her anchor.

With his experience and knowledge not only of the bay but of what had happened to the *Royal Charter* a century previously, he knew, none better, what little chance there was for the crew of the *Hindlea*. But he did what he could, and that in itself was enough to earn him the celebrated Gold Medal of the RNLI.

Quickly gathering together a skeleton crew of four, of whom one of them, volunteer Hugh Jones, had never even been out in a lifeboat before, Coxwain Richard Evans put out in a reserve boat, the *Edmund & Mary Robinson*. The official Moelfre lifeboat was being refitted.

There were waves twenty-five feet high and the winds were, as they had been on the night when the *Royal Charter* was lost, over a hundred miles an hour. In the teeth of this screaming hurricane, the valiant lifeboat discovered the *Hindlea* holding by one cable. Even though she was heading for certain destruction, the master would not give the signal to abandon ship until another hour and a half had passed, by which time the coaster was only two hundred yards from the rocks. The lifeboat had stood by, and as she moved to go to the assistance of the *Hindlea*, she was thrown onto her beam ends until the mast was under water.

She managed to right herself, and Coxwain Richard Evans tried a second time to approach the doomed ship. This time the lifeboat was hurled violently against the *Hindlea*'s side. Nothing daunted, however, Coxwain Evans tried no less than eight more times to approach the *Hindlea*, and each time, as the lifeboat went in, a member of the *Hindlea*'s crew managed to jump to safety.

Not a man was lost — not a member of the lifeboat's crew nor the lifeboat herself was lost — and all this accomplished in the spectacular maelstrom and fury of a raging gale. It was, most agreed, nothing short of a miracle — but a miracle which had required a very special sort of man to achieve.

Coxwain Evans went on to achieve the almost unheard-of distinction of in 1966 being awarded a second Gold Medal when he rescued ten men from the Greek freighter *Nafsiporos*, when she was in severe difficulties off the West Mouse — also in a hurricane! And as for the *Hindlea*, she was within a short time of the rescue, thrown with incredible force against the rocks and shattered. And there her remains lie still, a mere half-mile or so away from the wreck of the *Royal Charter*.

Chapter Twenty

Later Wrecks

Surprisingly, many of the later wrecks off the Welsh coasts have not occurred when the country was at war, but during peace-time. Little pleasure steamers, yachts, small vessels of all kinds, have come to grief in those deceptively calm seas, and we have heard the stories of many of them.

But of course, the two World Wars did play a large part in bringing many ships into danger. It was a peaceful Saturday afternoon in late February, 1915, for instance, and two little boys were gathering snowdrops on the cliffs near Amlwch when they heard a terrible explosion. What they witnessed as they ran to the edge to see what was happening, was the death of the 3,000-ton steamer *Cambank*, which had just been torpedoed off Point Lynas. She had taken on a pilot and was heading towards the Mersey when her crew saw the deadly periscope. What was left of her survivors were brought ashore by the Bull Bay lifeboat; the *Cambank* herself still lies where she went down.

This was extremely ironic, as in the same newspaper which reported the loss of the *Cambank* and four of her crew, was also reported Mr Winston Churchill's assurance to the Commons that Britain was ruler of the waves, and had swept every German ship from the seas. 'Significantly,' says historian Aled Eames, 'he did not refer to beneath the waves.'

Only a fortnight earlier, Lord Penrhyn's new steamer *Linda Blanche* had been sunk by the U-21 just eighteen miles from the Liverpool Bar Light-Vessel, but at least on this occasion, the U-boat had surfaced to allow the crew ten minutes to get into the boats before it sank Lord Penrhyn's ship! According to the local papers, the Germans had presented the crew of the *Linda Blanche* with cigars, behaved in an extremely friendly manner and even apologised for having to sink such an obviously new vessel (she had been at sea for just six months).

Such a gentlemanly attitude was not evident, however, in the encounter between the steamer *Sellagh* and another German submarine in February, 1917. The *Sellagh* was only one of six vessels sunk off Bardsey Island within a period of five days. She reported that she had been attacked by gunfire from the German which had killed the Chief Engineer and wounded other members of the crew, who had escaped in the boats only to see their vessel blow up by German bombs. The survivors were picked up by the steamer *Greenland* and landed at Holyhead. But only four days later, the *Greenland* in her turn was blown up off Bardsey. The other ships which were captured and sunk during the week in the same area — all by German submarines — were the 791-ton *Ferga*, the 375-ton *Margarita*, the 242-ton *Olivia* and the 564-ton *Kyanite*.

In contrast with the treatment which the emigrants had received when their vessels were wrecked off the Welsh coasts, the survivors of the *Sellagh, Ferga* and *Greenland* were, so Aled Eames tells us: 'landed in the port (of Holyhead) and fed and clothed before being sent home by rail'. Things had obviously taken a turn for the better from the point of view of survivors of shipwreck — their needs were now taken care of by the representatives of the Shipwrecked Mariners Society and shelter provided, in this area at least, by the Stanley Sailors' Home at Holyhead.

There were other sinkings, some within close range once again of Bardsey. The *Snowdon Ranger* was a mere twenty-five miles from the island when she was torpedoed with no warning in March. Her survivors claimed that the Germans, not satisfied with having killed four men in the torpedo attack, 'carried off all the provisions they could get hold of and finally sank her with bombs.'

They were in their boat for nearly ten hours until they were picked up by the SS *Somerset Court* and landed at Holyhead. The Superintendent of the Stanley Sailors' Home — now, doubtless, doing a roaring trade — added when he reported the incident: 'I have since heard of 6 Big Vessels which left Queenstown about the same time, only 2 got through and are now lying in the Roads.' A few days later, he was talking to the thirteen survivors of the SS *Crispin*, whose crew had numbered over a hundred men. They had also landed at Holyhead, very much the worse for wear after spending thirteen hours in an open boat, in bad weather.

A large number of ships were sunk off the Welsh coast, particularly Anglesey, during the last year or so of the First World War. The *Eskmere*, 2,293 tons, went down in September 1917, fifteen miles off South Stack. The *Apapa*, an even larger vessel of 7,832 tons, was sunk three miles from Point Lynas, and sixty-four survivors were brought to Holyhead. The *Apapa* had been en route from Lagos to Liverpool when she was torpedoed, and there must have been some heroic scenes during the early hours of the morning just after she was hit round about four o'clock.

For instance, it was recorded in the log-book of the Stanley Sailors' Home that one of the survivors was the 'son of the Station Master at Henley, who took charge of a child in one of the ship's boats who had had her arm blown away by the explosion.' Just one more of the many un-named heroes and heroines who were there in the aftermath of a wreck, on the spot when they were needed.

Nine vessels were sunk that December off Anglesey. Among them was the *Abgeri*, whose survivors once again landed in Holyhead. They included some naval personnel, who reported that the ship, which had been bound from Dacca to Liverpool, was sailing in convoy when she was torpedoed off Bardsey on Christmas Day. Escorting vessels had picked up those who survived, and one of these, P.56, which they believed was called a Decoy Ship, had destroyed the submarine and its crew. No-one from the submarine had been saved.

One after another, the torpedoed ships went down, and the sad little groups of survivors were landed on shore. There was a great deal of U-boat activity around the coasts, particularly in the later years of the war, when merchant ships began to travel in convoys, and the losses in the Atlantic and Western Approaches were reduced so dramatically, but the U-boats, looking round for other targets, attacked vessels sailing alone on inshore routes. The importance of Liverpool and the many vessels sailing to and from the port meant that there was, in particular, great activity around Anglesey.

In February, 1918, the *Mexico City* was sunk fifteen miles from

South Stack; two oil tankers, the *British Viscount* and the *Birchleaf*, went down two weeks later. During the first week in March, the *Penvearne* was torpedoed off South Stack, and twenty-two men were lost. The remaining survivors were brought in by the yacht *Vanessa*.

On the same day, the loss of the *Carmelite* and the *Kenmarc* were reported. The master of the *Kenmarc* was lost along with twenty-eight men; and only one survivor remained alive two days later from a crew of thirty-five in the *Romeo*.

The list seemed endless: the *Tarbetness*; the sailing vessel *Erica*, whose survivors managed to get ashore in their own boat; the Spanish ship *Arno Merndi*, which was torpedoed off South Stack just before midnight, leaving nine of her twenty-five man crew to make it to the shore on life-rafts. A few hours later, it was the turn of the *Cressida*, sixteen miles off the Skerries; and the same day the *Sea Gull* went down with the loss of her master and nineteen men.

The *Jane Gray*, an Amlwch schooner, was sunk by a U-boat off the Pembrokeshire coast, and at the end of March survivors of the cargo steamer *Conago* landed at Holyhead. When the *Conago*, which had remained afloat after being torpedoed, was boarded, the sad sight that greeted the eyes of the rescuers were dead bodies on deck — and a live South African ram, together with the ship's cat. Both animals were removed to safety, and attempts were made to tow the *Conago* but on the way, she was torpedoed once again, and this time sank off Holyhead.

Survivors from enemy U-boats were also brought in and the end of the U-boat reign came towards the close of 1918. There was much celebration and rejoicing all along the coast after the signing of the Armistice in November, and those who had survived the long and arduous period of war at sea paraded in thankfulness.

The same spirit of courage and indomitability pervaded these coasts during the Second World War. Aled Eames tells us that: 'On a stormy morning in August, 1941, in a strong S.W. gale, an aircraft crashed some way off the shore of Rhosneigr, and, unhesitatingly, there went into the sea to rescue the Polish airman ordinary people running from their everyday tasks, young boys, the coastguard, the local policeman, soldiers, airmen, a merchant seaman home on leave, in a tragic but vain attempt in which eleven of the would-be rescuers lost their lives.'

There had been, though, plenty of tragedies before this during the years of the war. Probably the best known loss was that of the submarine *Thetis*, the third of the new 'T' class submarines that had been ordered for the Royal Navy in 1936. After having been newly-launched on Thursday, June 1st, 1939, just before war had actually broken out, she went from the builder's yard at Birkenhead to carry out diving trials in Liverpool Bay.

There were 103 people on board, crew and technicians, one of them a Mersey pilot. The *Thetis* made an awkward first dive, taking fifty-eight minutes to overcome her buoyancy and then suddenly plunging beneath the waves. Attempts were made to contact her at ten-minute intervals when she failed to surface from her first dive, and all the resources of the Navy were rushed to the scene.

By 7.54 a.m. on the Friday morning, the *Thetis* was still underwater, and her escort vessels, which had wrongly calculated her position and their own, had lost her. It was the destroyer HMS *Brazen* which discovered her in the early morning, with her stern protruding from the sea for eighteen feet. The men within, trapped as they were, were contacted by underwater detonations to let them know help was standing by.

The lifeboat from Llandudno brought a doctor, and in the meantime, four men managed to escape from the *Thetis* by Davis apparatus through a hatch. But the remainder were weak from carbon dioxide poisoning and although the doctor waited all the rest of the day, as he said wryly, when commenting on the event: '. . . unfortunately my services were not needed.' The wire connecting the *Thetis* to the salvage ship which was standing by, broke and she sank very suddenly, or at least, it was assumed so, as she was not seen again for five months when she was eventually raised and refitted for war.

The ninety-nine men on board her were drowned, but when she was beached near Moelfre, their bodies were taken to Holyhead to be buried, and the *Thetis*, that ill-fated submarine, went back to the builder's yard to emerge later as HMS *Thunderbolt*, and to play an honourable part in the war. Just after the tragedy had occurred, the Llandudno lifeboat went back to the scene for a wreath to be cast on the surface of the sea, while the Last Post sounded from the accompanying HMS *Hebe*.

On April 14th, 1953, huge crowds gathered on the Menai Suspension Bridge watched the wrecking of the former 92-gun warship HMS *Conway* in the Menai Straits, while she was being towed to Liverpool for dry docking. Originally she had been launched as

HMS *Nile*, and on joining the Navy in April of 1854 she had been sent to the Gulf of Finland, where Britain was blockading the Russian fleet. She first visited the scene of her later career as a training vessel, Rock Ferry, in 1859. She moored next to the frigate HMS *Conway* which had just arrived on loan from the Admiralty to the Mercantile Marine Service Association, to be used as a cadet school for Merchant Navy officers.

With her own engines stripped away, the *Nile* was to return as the third training ship to bear the name HMS *Conway* to Rock Ferry on June 23rd, 1876. She was to stay there until May, 1941, when because of heavy air raids, she was towed to a berth in the Menai Straits for safety.

In 1949, she was the biggest vessel ever to pass from her berth near Bangor pier, to a new one off Plas Newydd, the eighteenth-century mansion which was to provide a shore base. The same procedure which had taken her safely under the suspension bridge and through the Swellies, was put into operation in reverse four years later to enable her to be towed to Liverpool for a refit. With two tugs in tow, she met her fate on this occasion when the currents in the Swellies brought her to a standstill and the towing line to one of the tugs parted. *Conway* drifted away and beached on the shore near the suspension bridge, breaking her back.

But that was not the end. Spectacularly, while being moved by a firm of salvage contractors three years later, she caught fire and burned to the waterline. The name of HMS *Conway* does, however, live on in a shore establishment in the grounds of Plas Newydd, which helps to provide accommodation for 316 cadets.

And even the wrecks of Wales are moving with the times. The link between terrified emigrants going down alongside mountains of Welsh slates on a sailing vessel and modern seamen battling for survival in their lifebelts, still holds if the stricken ship is something as futuristic as a hovercraft.

The first wreck of a hovercraft took place in Rhyl, where the vessel, which had been running a regular passenger service between Rhyl and Hoylake in 1962, was moored, waiting for a tug. When a storm blew up during the night of September 17, the mooring points were destroyed and the crew had to put to sea in order to save the craft from being driven onto the shore. The Rhyl lifeboat was launched in an effort to save the three-man crew.

A phenomenally high tide had caused the lifeboat house to flood to a depth of four feet, a thing that had never been heard of and never happened again, so the boat more or less launched itself straight off the promenade. The drifting hovercraft was located and the crew were able to jump to safety only minutes before she was completely wrecked — and the wreck must have been quite spectacular as she weighed 25 tons and was carrying 250 gallons of aviation fuel. The Coxwain, Harold Campini, was awarded the RNLI Silver Medal for successfully carrying out this dangerous mission.

It has been recorded that on many occasions, the survivors are loud in their applause and praise of all who sacrifice so much to try and save life from shipwreck. And of one thing we can be certain — that every time someone, somewhere off the Welsh coasts, is in danger and is snatched from the sea, the ghosts of all who have braved storm and hurricane and tempest in the long saga of Wales' historic shipwrecks, are there in the background, adding their own chorus of encouragement and approval.

Local Man Makes News

However terrible the wrecks which have taken place off the coasts of Wales, the ones which have caused the most distress to the Welsh people have been the ones where local men were involved. It is even claimed that when the *Titanic* went down with great loss of life, one Anglesey newspaper chose for its headline to announce this momentous event: 'Local man lost at sea'.

Selected Bibliography of Works Consulted

Dickens, Charles; *The Uncommercial Traveller* (Collins).

Eames, Aled; *Ships and Seamen of Anglesey 1558-1918* (The Anglesey Antiquarian Society, 1973).

Edmunds, George; *The Gower Coast* (Regional Publications, 1979).

Folklore, Myths and Legends of Britain (The Readers Digest Association Ltd, 1977).

Goddard, Ted; *Pembrokeshire Shipwrecks* (Christopher Davies, 1988).

Gruffydd, Elfed; *Ar Hyd Ben 'Rallt* (Pwllheli, 1991).

Haydock, Tim; *Treasure Trove: Where to find the great lost treasures of the world* (Fourth Estate, 1986).

Hudson, Kenneth and Nicholls, Ann; *The Book of Shipwrecks* (Macmillan, 1979).

Isle of Anglesey, Official Guide.

Jones, T. Llew; *Lawr ar Lan y Môr* (Gomer, Llandysul, 1977).

McKee, Alexander; *The Golden Wreck* (Souvenir Press, 1961).

Parry, Henry; *Wreck and Rescue on the Coast of Wales*

1. The Lifeboats of Cardigan Bay and Anglesey

2. The Story of the North Wales Lifeboats

(D. Bradford Barton Ltd, 1969 and 1973).

Phillips, Olive; *Gower* (Robert Hale, 1956).

Ross, J.E.; *Letters from Swansea* (Christopher Davies 1969).

Wynne Jones, Ivor; *Shipwrecks of North Wales* (David & Charles, 1973).